To Paul and Helen, my tree companions.
May we plant many more together.

Leaping Hare Press

First published in 2022 by Leaping Hare,
an imprint of The Quarto Group
The Old Brewery, 6 Blundell Street,
London N7 9BH,
United Kingdom
T (0)20 7700 6700

www.Quarto.com

A catalogue record for this book is available from the British Library.

ISBN 978-0-7112-7934-6
Ebook ISBN 978-0-7112-7935-3

9 8 7 6 5 4 3 2 1

Typeset in Minion Pro, Warnock Pro and Brandon Grotesque
Design: Tina Hobson
Commissioning editor: Monica Perdoni
Project editor: Michael Brunström

Printed in China

PLANT A TREE and RETREE THE WORLD

BEN RASKIN

CONTENTS

FORTY BEST TREES

TREES AND THE ECONOMY

INTRODUCTION

Trees evoke strong personal emotions in me, but when I look up beyond the canopy of branches, or down below the carpet of fallen leaves, I see that trees have a profound impact on our landscape, soils, wildlife and even climate. Sometimes described as the lungs of the planet, trees are crucial to the survival of our ecosystem and of us as species. Though they are technically oxygen-neutral over their lifetime (if you take into account what is released when they die and decompose), as they grow trees sequester carbon and are net oxygen producers. In recent decades we have removed huge areas of forest, and the world has suffered.

As a young boy, I made dens in the dense yew hedge in our garden, and climbed through the branches in the local park. In my professional career in horticulture, I have been lucky enough to plant and tend thousands of trees, and I am convinced they are the quickest and simplest method there is to mitigate against and adapt to climate change. They are, of course, neither a silver bullet nor the only answer but, along with reducing our consumption, planting trees is something we can all do as individuals to combat our climate crisis.

I live in a modest terraced cottage, with a relatively small garden. When we moved in, it had a couple of shrubs in one corner. It now has three apple trees and a fig tree trained against the fences, while dotted around the rest of the garden are a twisted hazel, a *Cornus kousa*, a black elder and a showy hibiscus. These are not big trees but they are all contributing to the health of my garden and planet, as well as bringing me joy and some lovely fruit.

Most people seem to love trees. They bring physical benefits such as shade, shelter and food, and also improve our happiness, boost our mental health and even reduce crime. Interacting with trees – and particularly climbing up them – has been shown to build confidence and resilience in children.

Our increasingly urban population has lost touch with trees. Despite loving nature and growing up right on the edge of a relatively small city with ready access to trees, I remained woefully ignorant about them until relatively recently. Apart from a few very common species, I couldn't identify many types of tree, and had no idea about how to harvest or use them. Once-commonplace skills, such as hedgelaying, coppicing and hurdle making, are now almost unknown, as we have rushed to replace almost everything we use with a cheap plastic version.

Farmers would once have valued the trees on their farms, using the wood for fuel, with the fruit and berries supplementing their cultivated crops. Before the advent of barbed wire and electric fencing, trees were a crucial way of making sure animals stayed where you wanted them. The global food market and constant downwards pressure on commodity prices have forced many farmers to simplify their farming systems, building scale and efficiency. Trees have been pushed out and marginalized. Hedges have been ripped from the landscape to allow for bigger machinery. Trees became a problem rather than an asset.

At the same time, forestry became more industrialized. Larger equipment and huge markets for biomass fuel and wood pulp have driven unsustainable practices in many areas. There is also the tragedy of the destruction of large areas of virgin forest, encouraged further by land clearance for soya and palm oil production.

Despite all this doom and gloom, the times are changing. Many countries are planting trees and incentivising more sustainable farming and forestry. Pioneering farmers and foresters are challenging the status quo and experimenting with regenerative food and timber systems. The role that trees could play to help climate change is also now well recognized, helping money to flow into replanting, both from governments and private companies. The integration of farming and trees (also called agroforestry), which is where I now spend most of my professional effort, is finally getting the recognition that it deserves as perhaps the most planet-friendly way of producing food.

This book aims to be both a celebration of trees and a call to action. Around fifteen years ago, I made a commitment to plant at least one tree every year for the rest of my life. I have so far done that, and more, almost all of it on other people's land. I don't own a farm, but I have not let this hold me back in my mission to bring more trees to the world. During my thirty years of work practising and advocating for organic and other earth-friendly production methods, I have never been more positive about the passion of people to save our planet, despite – or perhaps because of – the perilous conditions we have created.

If you already love trees, I urge you to protect them and increase their numbers. Become galvanized by groups such as the people of Sheffield, England, whose mass protest stopped a programme of urban tree removal. Or perhaps take as your inspiration, as I have, Jean Giono's wonderful story 'The Man Who Planted Trees'. Published in 1953, this fictional tale was way ahead of its time in showing the power that one man can have on the natural world. You could also look to the real-life Jadav Payeng, who has been leading a one-man forestry-planting crusade in India for more than forty years. Even if you have no space to plant trees where you live, you may still be able to get involved in community gardens and orchards, or even team up with local farmers to establish some tree planting on their land.

Planting trees is not the only way to play a crucial role, however. Many new forest and urban trees die from lack of care. Remove a tree tie as a young tree grows to prevent it from being strangled. Volunteer at a local park or woodland. Perhaps just try to buy your food from a farm that is planting trees. How we spend our time and money remains one of the most powerful tools we have for change

Just as we have, as a species, created the problems we are facing today, so humans can be part of the solution. One tree at a time.

TREES AND THE WORLD

TREES AND THE CLIMATE

Trees are widely recognized as one of the most important solutions to our climate crisis. They play a role both in mitigation and adaptation. There are, quite rightly, urgent campaigns and ambitious targets around the world to plant more trees. However, there is also the risk that in our rush to retree the world we will do the wrong thing. I'll take a look here at how trees help our climate, and what we might need to be wary of.

Carbon sequestration

This is the big one. Trees (like all photosynthesising plants) take carbon dioxide from the air and use it to produce carbohydrates. What happens to this sequestered carbon, though? Some of it goes into the wood of the tree. This carbon is fixed in the timber until such time as the wood rots or is burnt. At this point it is released back into the air. Much of the carbohydrate produced by plants, however, is exuded through their roots to feed soil organisms. This is part of a complicated symbiotic relationship between tree roots and the soil ecosystem. Sugars, which nonphotosynthesising animals can't produce, are traded for other nutrients that a plant needs to access in a soluble form from the soil. Much of this soil carbon is in constant flux, as animals eat each other and excrete, absorbing and releasing carbon. An increase in soil life (and particularly in fungi, as we shall see on pages 21–24) will result in a reduction in carbon dioxide in the air, but it is less stable than that held in a tree, and can be released by soil disturbance or application of some agrochemicals, and especially fungicides.

If we can increase tree cover in the world, we should be able to reduce the amount of carbon dioxide in the atmosphere. However, this does depend on the types of trees we choose, and how we plant and manage them. It also depends on where in the world we plant. Trees grow quickest in the tropics, and some argue that planting in the UK and other temperate zones is likely to have only a marginal effect on carbon dioxide levels. Trees planted in areas that might otherwise be snow-covered could even have a negative effect, as they are dark and therefore absorb light and are warmer than the white ice or snow.

A big tree will, in theory, sequester more carbon, but it might take longer to do so. Coppicing a tree keeps it in a state of juvenility and quick growth, so this could pull more carbon dioxide out of the air, but it depends on what you do with the coppiced growth. Burning wood as biofuel just releases the carbon straight back into the atmosphere, though if that fuel is replacing fossil fuel there might still be some net advantage.

There are also lots of unknowns about the longer-term effects of planting in a particular place. For example, planting lots of trees in a very dry area might result in further water shortages, or it might stimulate a shift in weather patterns that attracts rain and transforms the local ecosystem. It is also important not to view this only through a carbon lens. Biodiversity, continuing food production and social justice are also crucial. However, the potential is huge. A 2019 study estimated that there are 1.7 billion hectares of land not growing crops that could be planted with trees. The study did include currently grazed land, and rightly so. Though planting new forests will have a carbon benefit, the highest gains, in my opinion, are likely to come from planting trees where they can improve a whole farm or ecosystem. Agroforestry is one such powerful example, examined in more depth on pages 31–5.

Water management

One consequence of climate change appears to be increasingly extreme and erratic weather. Rain comes less frequently, but in greater quantities. This makes life difficult for both farmers and communities. The faster rain falls from the sky, the more likely it is to run off the surface and down into streams, rivers and roads, overwhelming the ability of the drainage system to cope. Farmers lose their soil, river beds get silted up and localized flooding causes misery to communities.

Improving the health of our soils generally can help, since increased soil carbon and health means that the soil can hold more water. The sticky excretions of worms and other soil organisms also help to clump soil particles together, giving them strength when pounded by the deluge. This is also beneficial during dry spells, when the organic matter in soil absorbs and traps water, giving a slow release and enabling better plant growth.

As well as building organic matter in the soil, trees have a further stabilizing influence on water. They improve the infiltration of water through the soil, so when we get long, heavy rain, more of the water is absorbed into the deeper soil levels and escapes slowly, rather than running off the surface and quickly into streams and rivers. Many upland areas in the UK, for instance, are grazed by sheep, leading to short grass and surface soil compaction, both of which stop water seeping into the soil. A group of farmers in Wales worked together at a landscape scale and planted trees to tackle this problem. Known as the Pont Bren Project, their tree-planting reduced surface run-off in one area by sixty times compared to the area with no trees just 10 km (6¼ miles) away.

Rewilding

Rewidling is currently a fashionable term, and one that on the face of it has a lot to offer. The concept is that you stop managing land and allow nature to reclaim it. Biodiversity returns, plants and trees grow, and all for minimal effort and energy. There are some powerful examples of where this has worked, such as Knepp Estate in the UK, who transformed a loss-making arable farm into what they call a 'wildland', effectively managed by free-roaming livestock from which they harvest a percentage for meat sales. They have seen a staggering increase in soil health, biodiversity and tree growth over a surprisingly short time. What would happen if we turned the whole world over in this way? Could it solve our problems? It is great from a wildlife and carbon perspective, but we do need to grow crops in order to feed people. It is also likely that not all land would respond in the same way.

There is a worrying trend worldwide for private companies, funded by carbon or biodiversity offsetting money, to buy land from struggling marginal farmers and then either plant forests or leave them to rewild. Why is this a problem? In my opinion, there are two major flaws to the approach. Firstly, it allows companies that are causing environmental harm to continue doing that harm without tackling the root of the problem. While many companies are genuinely trying to change the way they operate, many are not and use offsets as 'greenwash'. Secondly, it marginalizes and ignores the indigenous people currently occupying the land. It is another form of colonialism. Tree planting and/or rewilding certainly have their place, but they need to be implemented by existing communities, farmers and farming practices in a fair and appropriate manner.

TREES, SOIL AND FUNGI

Adding trees and uncultivated areas of ground into farms and gardens helps to pull carbon from the atmosphere and into plant material and soils. To understand this more fully, we'll take a step back and look at how soil is formed.

The process often starts with bare rock, after a volcanic eruption or the retreat of a glacier, for instance. The first organisms to colonize this naked rock tend to be bacteria and lichens. They are able to break down the rock chemically and release nutrients through excretion and death, allowing other more complex plants and fungi to form. As the soil ages, particularly when trees, shrubs and other perennial plants take hold, the fungal proportion of the soil increases compared to bacteria. This is called the fungi:bacteria ratio. Your vegetable beds might have a ratio of 1:1, while a conifer forest could have a ratio of 1,000:1. This symbiotic relationship between trees and fungi is key in understanding both the potential benefits and how best to establish new plantings.

Fungi can be huge. The largest recorded organism on the planet is thought to be a 2,500-year-old *Armillaria ostoyae* fungus in the Malheur National Forest in Oregon. It has colonized more than 8 km² (3 square miles). This is impressive in its own right, but the potential it offers to other organisms is equally amazing. The fungus can transport a range of nutrients through its miles of mycelium and trade them with trees for sugars. The more fungi there are, the greater the area from which a tree can access minerals to help it grow.

Since trees prefer a fungal soil, you can help them establish and grow quickly by giving them a good woodchip mulch (see page 69). Woodchip is an easily digestible superboost for soil fungi. When wood is chipped, it cuts across the wood fibres that run along the branch or trunk. Fungi finds it less difficult to enter through the open cut and quickly starts breaking down the wood.

How trees benefit soil

Though we all love trees, they are not necessarily the right answer for all soils. Grasslands can sequester as much or even more carbon than woodlands, and for certain soils or landscapes they are better for biodiversity. However, assuming we're planting in the right place, trees build soil health and quality in a number of ways apart from just photosynthesising and adding to soil organic matter.

Firstly, they recycle nutrients from lower levels of the soil. Their deep roots reach down further than those of smaller plants and can mine minerals from the subsoil, which they pump up through their trunks into leaves and branches. As these die and fall, they are broken down and added into the mineral content of the upper soil layer. These nutrients are key to the health of soil organisms, plants and even those species that then feed on plants and animals. Humans, for instance, are thought to require more than 130 different nutrients to reach peak health (if there is such a thing). Almost all of these will come from the breakdown of soil minerals, with some being blown on the wind or washed in with the rain.

However careful we are to provide cover to our soils, there are inevitably times of year in most farming and gardening when we have to disturb the ground. When soil is bare it is vulnerable to erosion from either wind or rain. Light soils are particularly at risk. Old photographs of the dust bowls in America are a perfect illustration of what can happen when there is no shelter from wind in large areas of unprotected soil. Trees can really help. They provide a physical barrier that slows the wind down and prevents it from blasting soil into the hedges or further afield. At the other end of the weather extreme, tree roots create channels in the soil that allow water to percolate quickly into the soil. This reduces surface flooding, keeping the soil in the field where it should be, and even helping to prevent local flooding by slowing the release of water from higher ground to the valleys below.

When the water does eventually drain from the field, the evidence shows that it is cleaner. The improved soil and drainage created by the trees provide a natural filtration system that absorbs soluble nutrients such as nitrates and phosphates, as well the tiny participates that can clog up the spawning ground in gravel river beds.

TREES AND WILDLIFE

What do trees do for wildlife, and do more trees always mean greater biodiversity? In an area denuded of woodland planting, new trees will help restore some of what has been lost. This is equally true in cities, much of our farmed environment and in regions where land has desertified. When done wrong, however, tree-planting can have a net-negative effect on wildlife. Converting a species-rich ancient meadow to woodland would be a disaster, for instance. Similarly, planting peat bogs with trees might mean destroying fragile wetlands and releasing carbon. Monocultures of quick-growing conifer species do not provide the complex diversity of habitats needed to support diverse ecological communities. Fortunately, forward-thinking foresters have been moving towards a more enlightened approach, as for instance laid out by Clive Thomas, my colleague at the Soil Association, in its 2022 Regenerative Forestry report.

For the purpose of this book, I will assume we are planting the right tree in the right place, and explore some of the opportunities we have to increase our wildlife, mostly in gardens, public spaces and farms.

Trees for food

Since they are the parts of the tree we normally eat, it is straightforward for us to imagine fruit and nuts helping out wildlife too, and this is certainly the case. Some creatures, like birds, fly in to feed on berries and seeds. Squirrels and monkeys climb up for fruit and nuts, while animals like pigs browse on fallen gifts on the forest floor. Choosing trees that give over as long a period as possible will help to support more wildlife. Hawthorn, for example, tends to hang on to its berries well into the winter, while a crab apple will usually drop its fruit sooner.

At the start of the year, before there are any fruiting bodies, tree flowers are an important source of nectar for insects and some birds. Trees often flower earlier than herbaceous or annual plants, so provide food for creatures as soon as the weather starts to warm up after winter. Willow, magnolia and blackthorn are just a few of the earliest flowers to help feed wildlife.

There are lots of animals that feed on the leaves, shoots and bark of trees. Koalas are famous for eating exclusively eucalyptus, but I know from experience that deer, rabbits and hares, and pretty much any herbivore, will nibble at tree leaves. Some are much tastier than others. The more bitter the leaf, the less likely it is to be browsed. So trees like willow, lime and mulberry are often the first to be snacked on, while walnuts will be left until there is nothing else to eat. In winter, when food is scarce, many ground-living creatures will eat the bark of young trees, as it is the only living thing poking its head above the snow and ice. So while you may be more than happy to support wildlife, good tree guards are essential to make sure your young trees survive.

Trees for habitat

Trees are not just great for eating; they also provide crucial homes for creatures. Nesting birds and mammals find a safe, dry place to lay eggs or bring up their young. Some caterpillars curl leaves around them to hide from predators, while a host of tiny insects, such as ants, mites and aphids, hide in the cracks of bark or between the nodes of twigs and branches. Different types of woodland support different species too. Lichens, for instance, don't do well in dense forests and woodland, which are too dark for them to do well. Lichens are incredible organisms, a sort of composite organism of algae and fungi. They need both a surface to grow on, such as trees or stone, and sunlight. Wood pasture is a habitat with some trees and some open spaces, allowing for a mix of grasses and low-growing plants and trees. It is perfectly suited to lichens. Mosses, too, do well in wood pasture, but they can also cope with the shadier conditions of denser woodland. Woodland that has a mix of deciduous and evergreen species is likely to support the widest range of flora and fauna.

Complex systems

Even once trees die, their branches and trunks continue to provide food and habitat. Beetles, for example, often rely on rotting trunks to feed their larval stage. The stag beetle can live up to five years as a larva before metamorphosis, so needs a good supply of large rotting logs. Leaving log piles around in gardens and parks is a great way to support wildlife. Tidy is the enemy of life.

In my work on farms planting trees for agroforestry systems, I have observed two important things. The first is how quickly wildlife increases once you start planting trees. Within six months of planting one field, we saw a dramatic increase in birds of prey. Barn owls, kestrels, buzzards and red kites, which had been occasional visitors when the field was a sheep grazed paddock, became commonplace. This was largely due to the increase in voles. While we had some tree damage, they mostly seemed to eat other leaves, seeds and roots from the mixed grasses and legumes in the sward. The other observation was that it is not just the trees that make a difference, but the change of the whole system brought about by the trees. In the same field, we saw orchids return after three years, because we stopped continuous grazing and started cutting once or twice a year.

If we create complex systems, with a diversity of habitats, longer grass, trees to hide in, lines of trees that provide hunting grounds for the raptors, a change in soil with more organic matter, better drainage and higher organic matter, we will support a greater number of species of all sizes. We can all play a part in promoting this complexity. Leave some logs in the corner of your garden or petition your local authorities to leave areas wild and plant trees in areas that are just mown lawn. Perhaps you can sponsor a tree with a local farm, or try to buy your food from farms that are planting more trees. There is now a market stall in Borough Market in London that specializes in selling products from farms practising agroforestry.

AGROFORESTRY

Agroforestry is the term given to the deliberate mixing of trees and farm enterprises – livestock or crops. In modern farming we are used to seeing big fields of corn or sheep, while woodland and forest are seen as separate. This was not always the case. Before the invention of large agricultural machinery, small fields and diverse systems were the norm. As farming kit has become bigger and farms have specialized, this exile of trees and shrubs to the periphery has reached the point where huge swathes of countryside are now treeless. It doesn't need to be this way though. Many areas of the world still practice polyculture (another name for diverse, mixed farming systems) and agroforestry is making a big comeback.

How do trees help farming?

It seems counterintuitive. You would imagine that trees would take land out of production. However, farming with trees is likely to increase overall productivity by at least 30 per cent, and in addition will make the farm more resilient to both climate change and market forces. There are such a wide range of benefits it would need a whole book to outline them all, but here are just a few: improved soil health, increased biodiversity, soil moisture management, better animal health and welfare, temperature modulation and income diversity. Many of these benefits come just from having the trees on your land, but of course trees also produce things that can be sold to make them profitable in their own right. Nuts, fruit, timber and woodchip are just some of the ways to get food or income from trees to supplement the more traditional farming enterprise of livestock and crops.

The basic principle of agroforestry is that farming with trees maximizes the 'free' resources that farmers rely on: sunlight, water and soil. Let's take each of those in turn.

Sunlight – Every ray of sunshine that falls onto bare soil is wasted; either absorbed as heat or reflected back into the atmosphere. If, instead, that light hits a leaf, the energy is used by the plant to create sugars that can feed not only itself but organisms in the soil and then up the food chain to grazing animals and people. Most of our annual crops are short-lived and need planting into bare soil, so for much of the year the surface of the ground is barely covered, leading to massive waste of solar energy. Including trees – which are typically in leaf for longer than crops, and grow higher

– within the cropped area increases the sunlight captured and therefore the productivity of the farm.

Soil – Trees have deeper roots than annual plants or perennial grasses. They are able to tap into the mineral resources of soils at a greater depth and bring those nutrients up through their leaves, which they then drop onto the top layer of soil. This increases the carbon level and health of the soil, leading to greater productivity. Though there is some competition between crops and trees, research has shown that in many cases the disturbance of the soil at the surface for growing crops, forces the trees roots lower enabling even better use of the lower soil resource.

Water – Rain doesn't come exactly when you need it. Often we have either too much or too little. Conserving water during dry spells and being able to quickly dispel deluges is a huge benefit to a farmer. Planting trees improves the structure of the soil through increased organic matter, which acts like a sponge in dry weather, holding on to more water for a longer period. Conversely the deep roots create drainage channels which allow water to infiltrate quickly down to the lower soil levels helping to reduce flooding. Trees can transpire as much as 2,000 litres (440 gallons) of water a day, so they can really help to pull water out of saturated soils.

How trees help animals

If you have ever been caught out in cold driving rain or bright searing heat, you will know that the best place to be is protected under a big tree. Animals are the same; they are happier and more productive when protected from extremes of temperature. Any energy they don't need to use to keep warm they can put into producing milk or meat. Similarly, in very hot weather their normal functions can slow down or pause. Most of our domesticated animals are originally from wooded pasture habitats, and are not only more healthy but mentally happier when trees are present.

Browsing on trees is also great for animal health. Tree leaves tend to have much higher levels of micronutrients than grasses, and higher tannin levels, which can help to reduce internal parasites. Some trees, like willow, even have medicinal values that animals will actively seek out when feeling unwell. In very hot weather, many grasses stop growing as the top layer of soil runs out of moisture. In the very hot year of 2018, we noticed that the only area on the farm where the grass was growing was in the shade of the trees. However, there is often still plenty of moisture further down the soil profile that trees can access, so trees can provide very useful summer food. We are now actively planting areas of trees or 'browsing blocks' to give the animals something to eat when the grass gives up.

Many farmers worry that having too many trees will mean their grass won't grow. The science though shows the exact opposite, with most grass and forage species growing better in the shade, even at quite high levels of cover. Not only that, but trees provide shelter from wind, resulting in about a 5 per cent higher temperature, so grass starts growing earlier in the year and keeps growing later, sometimes giving four to six weeks extra grazing for animals.

Trees can help save our planet, I'd even go so far as to say that we won't survive as a species without them. But we need to value them more highly. Planting more trees is great and vital, but we also should use them more sustainably. Later in the book we'll look about how that could be good for the economy too.

TREES AND HAPPINESS

SHADE AND SHELTER

Why do we love trees so much? At a very basic level, perhaps we subconsciously understand that trees offer us protection. Although we no longer need them to escape predators, we still turn to them for refuge in weather extremes. I am sure we have all rested under cooling branches in a hot summer or taken cover from a downpour. In my work with animals and trees, I have come to learn more about the science behind how animals use trees to their benefit and the same is true for us.

Temperature modulation

You'll know the phrase 'wind chill factor', which refers to the effect of the wind making it feel like it is colder than it actually is. Depending on wind speed, the shelter of a hedge or thick trees can reduce that factor, leading to a typical temperature increase of 5°C (9°F).

In very hot weather, trees have a cooling effect, not just when we stand in their direct shade, but in the area around them too. They do this both by intercepting the sunlight and by evapotranspiration, which has a similar effect to when we sweat. The area under trees can be 11–25°C (20–45°F) cooler than the highest temperatures in full sun. The more trees you have in an area, the cooler it will be. When we are very hot, our bodies don't function so well. The WHO (World Health Organization) warns that 'Even small differences from seasonal average temperatures are associated with increased illness and death. Temperature extremes can also worsen chronic conditions, including cardiovascular, respiratory and cerebrovascular disease and diabetes-related conditions.' So cooling our environment down in the summer is not just about comfort, but will have an impact on health and potentially reduce hospitalizations.

Planting trees to reduce your energy bills

Planting trees not only draws carbon out of the atmosphere; it can also help to reduce the amount we release in keeping ourselves comfortable. If we lower the wind chill factor in the vicinity of our house, we will not need to use so much energy heating it. And if we have our house partly in shade, the air conditioning will run more efficiently. Houses that don't have air conditioning will simply be more pleasant when shaded in the summer.

To keep your house warmer, the main aim is to reduce air speed. Wind will take heat away from your house more quickly. Work out where your cold winds come from and plant on that side of the house for maximum protection. Evergreen trees are more effective, since they keep their leaves in the winter and provide a more useful block. However, it gets a bit more complicated since you can get an eddying effect on the sheltered side of the windbreak as the air flows over the top. A semi-permeable barrier with some deciduous and some evergreen can be more effective. Also, take into account the shading effect of evergreen trees if planted near the house. You don't want to lose the warming effect of winter sun in your efforts to keep out the wind.

To keep your house cooler in summer you want deciduous trees that will give shade from overhead sun but won't darken and cool in the winter. Plant them to give morning shade from the east and afternoon shade from the west. Even once they have lost their leaves, trees will still cast some shadow, so don't plant them too near the house. Keeping air conditioning units in shade will make them run more efficiently, though only if air movement is not restricted. Smaller trees with lower branches pruned are a good option.

TREES AND POLLUTION

Though the move toward electric cars will help enormously in reducing air pollution in cities, there are plenty of other sources beyond petrol and diesel engines that will continue to pose a health threat for decades to come. Car tyres, industrial and construction emissions and even particulates from fireworks, are just a few of the threats to our health. Air pollution is known to cause or inflame respiratory problems such as asthma, and can also increase the risk of strokes, lung cancer and heart disease. Ioannis Bakolis of King's College, London, has recently looked at how air pollution is linked to a rise in a range of mental illnesses. While reducing the source of pollution is obviously preferable, in the meantime trees are a great natural ally in helping mitigate this problem.

Trees provide a physical block. When a cloud of polluted air hits a tree, firstly it will get broken up and become less concentrated. Secondly, a proportion of the contamination will stick to the tree, in its rough bark or hairy leaves. Most of this will then be washed off into the soil or drainage system when it rains – not great for the soil but at least it is not getting directly into our lungs.

Trees have one more trick up their leaves. They are able to filter some atmospheric pollutants such as ammonia, sulphur dioxide and nitrogen dioxide through the stomata in their leaves. As we have already seen, trees also lower temperatures in urban areas, which decreases the risk of harmful pollutants that are worse on hot days, for instance ground-level ozone. A final positive side-effect of a tree barrier is that it also absorbs sound, so can reduce noise pollution.

Nothing is ever simple in nature, so choosing the right tree to reduce pollution is not easy. Trees with rough, hairy leaves, like silver birch and elder, tend to be good at capturing airborne particulates. There are some super-robust species, like London plane or honey locust, but generally deciduous trees are less effective as they lose their leaves, and hence their superpower, in the winter. However, conifers can sometimes give off chemicals that mix with car exhaust to produce ozone. Conifers tend to be more susceptible to damage from salt, which is a problem in colder regions that regularly need to de-ice roads. And evergreen species also block out winter light. If we can get it right, though, planting more trees in urban areas will reduce air pollution.

WHY CLIMBING TREES IS GOOD FOR YOU

The online world is expanding quickly, offering a growing volume of information and involvement in the virtual world. At the same time, our real-life experiences seem to be shrinking. Children can play computer games with friends across the world, but they often have no access to green spaces and unstructured play, and most parents feel nervous about letting their children play unsupervised in the streets.

Though now more than half a century old, I still love hoofing it up a tree and seeing the world from a different perspective. Perhaps, like swimming, climbing is an innate evolutionary desire, inherited from our monkey ancestors. However, climbing trees is not just fun; it teaches us some fundamentals about how to approach life.

Assessing risk is a vital skill and one that takes some time to learn. Some of this learning can happen at a playground on climbing frames, but this is still a managed environment with fewer variables, and often a soft, less risky, surface to fall to. You can, of course, get hurt climbing a tree, from a scratch or cut to broken bones or worse. However, with some basic climbing checks and simple rules, the risks can mostly be eliminated. For instance, teach your kids to look for dead wood, make sure they don't stand on branches thinner than their legs and get them to practise coming down before they climb too high. The confidence gained from a good tree climb can help in other situations.

Though I have long believed in giving my children permission to explore, I was delighted to find some science to back up my views. Carla Gull and her team from the University of Phoenix, Arizona, carried out a study that looked at the benefits and risks of tree climbing on child development and resiliency, and found that although it might result in minor injury, 'children afforded the opportunity to be involved in risky play such as tree climbing have the potential to grow socially, emotionally, physically, cognitively and creatively, and have increased resiliency'.

In early societies that relied on hunting and gathering, climbing trees was an essential part of survival, so it is one that we are well adapted to as a species. A clamber up the trunk to gather fruit or wild honey, or to escape a predator, needs a degree of confidence and competency. While we may not need those specific skills to survive modern city life, it seems we still benefit in a range of ways when we climb.

Gull also concluded that 'bans on tree climbing and other risky play pose problems such as limiting access to natural spaces, creating fear of participation in adventurous activities, and fewer opportunities to negotiate risk and develop resiliency'.

Finding trees to climb is not always easy. Most of us cannot boast our own climable tree, and even those of us lucky enough to have a garden probably do not have a suitable climbing tree in it. Parks and accessible woodlands are the best place to start. In the UK, the National Trust has properties around the country and actively encourages children to play in their trees.

How to climb a tree: a few simple rules

Inspection – Check the tree is not rotten and that there are no nesting animals in it. Early spring to late summer are when most birds nest but best to make sure at any time of the year.

Keep it light – Take off any loose coats or backpacks; you don't want to get caught on any branches.

Don't climb on your own – If you fall, you'll need somebody to get help. For the same reason, it's best not to all climb at once. In smaller trees you might get in each other's way but even if you are up a big tree, having someone on the ground can be useful to guide you down.

EXPANDING TREE-BASED PLAY

Climbing may be the gold standard when it comes to messing about in trees, but it is not always possible. Kids may not have access to a big enough tree, be too young, or perhaps not have the confidence or physical ability. This doesn't rule out tree play, though, so let's explore a few more ways we can use trees (both alive and dead) to expand our play and exploration of the world.

Treehouses

If you are lucky enough to have a suitable tree in your garden, you can build a treehouse. This can be as simple as a wooden platform. If the tree and your ambition are large enough, you can add walls and a roof to make a perfect hideaway or play setting. Even if you don't have a suitable tree, you can still build a treehouse. I made one for my kids on my allotment next to a small tree, out of old pallets and a salvaged stepladder. It gave them a sense of being up in the trees and they spent many happy hours playing. Lots of adults and children like to have a secret place where they can escape the troubles of their daily lives. If it is up a tree then so much the better.

Using dead bits of tree

Using fallen branches or logs to create play areas is also a great way to build imagination in kids' play. Logs laid lengthways, or in cross-sections to provide stepping-stones of various heights, can be cheap way to create an adventure playground in your garden for even the youngest of children. Those with a little creative flair and carpentry skills can use dead trunks and branches to make 'jungle gyms', with places to swing or rope ladders. If you treat the wood (there are eco wood preservers on the market), these branches should last a few years, especially if you choose a hard, resilient wood like oak or chestnut. Jumping, balancing or even looking for little creatures in the bark are all ways that we can explore nature and learn about the world around us.

Storytelling and history

Trees have long held a powerful place in our myths and stories. How many fairy tales have trees as a central part of the story? From Sleeping Beauty's thicket of thorns to Robin Hood, or legends like Yggdrasil the Norse tree of life and the whispering oak of Dodona in Greek mythology, trees are intertwined with our cultural identities. We can build on these traditions and create our own stories among trees. I love imagining how long trees have been there and what type of people might have seen them or sat under their branches. Speculating how many have passed beneath a 500-year-old yew tree by a churchyard – and that it might still be living in another 500 years long after we have died – gives a new perspective for children who live largely in the moment.

TREES AND MENTAL HEALTH

Mental wellbeing is finally getting the attention it deserves, though we are a long way from fully understanding all that causes or remedies mental health problems. Being in nature and specifically around trees, however, is something that has been proven to have a positive effect for many people. Trees have the power to reduce stress and anxiety, so increasing your contact with trees could make you a happier person. But how do they do it?

In addition to the enjoyment that comes from the peace and beauty of being out in the woods, trees release phytoncides. These are a large number of volatile chemicals that trees use to deter pests and disease. When we breathe them in, however, they have been shown to have a positive effect on our health. One way they do this is by boosting the production in our bodies of what are called NK ('natural killer') cells. These are the cells that work for us against disease, for instance fighting cancer. Phytoncides can also reduce inflammation, lower our levels of cortisol (the hormone associated with stress) and even help with sleep. With all of that going on in, it's no surprise that we feel better under a leafy canopy.

Even a Christmas tree will emit some phytoncides: another reason to favour a real tree over plastic.

In Japan in the 1980s, a concept called 'forest bathing' was developed, which captures this idea of tapping into the restorative power of trees. What I like about this idea is that it brings positivity and purpose to what might otherwise be seen as just going for a walk. It challenges the tendency to reach immediately for a pharmaceutical solution and empowers those suffering to find part of their cure in their own neighbourhood. The scientific evidence backs this up. Among many studies, one in Japan showed that:

> ... walking through forest areas decreased the negative moods of 'depression-dejection', 'tension-anxiety', 'anger-hostility', 'fatigue' and 'confusion' and improved the participants' positive mood of 'vigour', compared with walking through city areas.

TREES, COMMUNITY AND REDUCED CRIME

Despite my deep love of trees, I confess I had never considered their potential impact on crime. Indeed, many people would say they feel more vulnerable in a wooded environment than in an open one with no trees. However, there is evidence that in urban areas planting trees can contribute to a reduction in violence and crime.

A study by Frances Kuo and William Sullivan from the University of Illinois found that more trees could mean less criminal behaviour. Though complicated, they believe there may be a couple of main influences at work. Firstly, where there are trees you'll find more people. People love being around trees. Kuo and Sullivan found that 83 per cent more people socialized in their trial treed area than in barren spaces. This was especially true of children, who were much more likely to come out and play in a natural, well treed environment. More people out on the streets led to less crime.

Secondly, there may be a longer-term benefit from socializing and community-building that further reduces crime. If you know your neighbours well and feel emotionally connected, you are more likely to look out for them or call them if you are in trouble. There has also been the suggestion that a treed and green environment looks more cared for than a barren, paved area and is therefore less attractive to potential criminals.

The other interesting finding from this study was that improved mental health – and particularly the reduced stress and mental fatigue that trees provide – lowered aggression in those that lived in buildings surrounded by trees. It is thought that the trees provide a similar function to activities such as meditation or yoga. It is well known that animals kept in unnatural and barren conditions are unhappy and can develop aggressive or depressive behaviour. Well guess what? Humans are the same.

Another study, published in *Landscape and Urban Planning*, estimated that in Baltimore, Maryland, 'a 10 per cent increase in tree canopy was associated with a roughly 12 per cent decrease in crime', and very interestingly that the association was stronger for trees planted on public land than for those on private property, though in all but a few isolated instances there was some positive correlation between trees and crime reduction. Barren areas were seen almost as 'no man's land'; nobody felt responsible or attached to them, and as such could become part of a gang's territory. Trees, conversely, were seen to be boundary markers, signalling the beginning of a different neighbourhood.

I am lucky enough to live in the countryside with trees all around. For the majority of the planet who live in towns and cities, trees can still and should play a major part in our lives. Filtering pollution, cooling and warming and just looking beautiful, trees are essential. If you don't already, take some time as you go about your life to look more closely at trees. Imagine how they live and survive, and consider giving them something back for all the good they bring to us.

GROWING
TREES

RAISING YOUR OWN TREES

There's nothing wrong with buying a tree, but there is something special about growing your own, and for many species it is not hard. You'll first need to check the best way to propagate your chosen tree. Let's look here at three basic methods: growing from seed, taking cuttings and grafting.

Growing from seed

This is the cheapest method. You can collect or cheaply buy hundreds of seeds for most naturally occurring trees. Some species, such as oaks, will germinate very quickly; indeed, you have to sow them soon after they fall from the tree. Others, like the spindle tree, will only germinate after specific seed pre-treatments, including stratifying, the term given to operations such as soaking or scratching the seed, or periods of cold temperatures that help the germination process.

If you are collecting seed, make sure you have the landowner's permission. If you are lucky they will also be a tree lover and will be delighted to have some extra trees grown in return for the seed. The beauty of this method is that you will end up with a genetically unique tree, the first of its kind.

Taking cuttings

A few trees will grow from cuttings, or pieces of stem or root. These are effectively clones, so will be genetically identical to the plant you took the cutting from. Willow is the easiest to propagate by this method. Trees that sucker from the base of their stem also tend to root easily. For stem cuttings, simply take a piece of the stem approximately 15 cm (6 in) long, and either put it in water or in a moist compost until roots begin to sprout, then plant it into the ground, or grow it in a pot until it is bigger, and then plant out. For root cuttings, it is best to plant the cutting into a pot or a tray of compost. Once shoots start to appear you know it has been successful.

Grafting

This method is a little more complicated and, like taking cuttings, is great if you want an exact replica of the parent plant, for instance a particular variety of fruit. You take a stem cutting (a 'scion') from the mother plant of your choice, and then join it to a different but compatible rootstock. Rootstocks are normally chosen to give a particular characteristic, such as size, disease resistance or temperature tolerance. To ensure a good union between scion and rootstock, a commonly used technique when starting out is the 'whip-and-tongue' method. The key is to ensure the cambium layers (the layer a few cells thick just under the bark) are lined up. Without good contact the actively dividing cells within both parts of the tree are unable to fuse and grow.

Growing them on

You'll probably need to grow your tree on a bit before planting it out. This is particularly important if you have pests like rabbits or deer that love munching on little saplings. If you have just a few trees then a big pot or a protected area in your garden will work fine. If you are growing large numbers of trees you can fill troughs or trays with compost, or set out an area in the soil which is then protected from pests and wind. Newly growing trees like rich soil and hate drying out, so a good mulch of compost or woodchip is an ideal way to protect and feed the roots. You may well need to water them in dry weather. After one year of growing they should be big enough to plant out into their final positions.

GROWING APPLE TREES ON THEIR OWN ROOTS

There are some very good reasons for using a different rootstock for your trees. However, there is also a potential downside. Graft incompatibility is what happens when the scion and rootstock don't match closely enough. For instance, you can't graft an apple variety onto a cherry rootstock. Even if you graft one apple onto another, there will be a degree of incompatibility. The swelling around the graft on a tree you sometimes see is one sign of that.

I was fortunate enough to work with Hugh Ermen, a phenomenal apple breeder in the UK. Hugh firmly believed that growing apples on their own rootstocks (in other words, ungrafted) led to a healthier, stronger plant with improved fruit set and fruit quality. My limited experience in growing ungrafted trees has supported this view. The problem though is that apples don't easily root from stem cuttings. This makes starting your own trees a little more complicated, though certainly not impossible. Once you have one tree growing on its own roots, you can propagate more of them from root cuttings.

Establishing an own-root apple tree

First, graft your chosen variety onto the weakest, most dwarfing rootstock you can get your hands on, for instance an M27. Grow on as normal for the first year to get the plant established. In early spring plant the tree in a bigger pot with the graft union buried under the surface. This will allow the main variety to root into the soil – something you would normally be trying to avoid of course. Most varieties have fairly vigorous root systems and so will send out roots quickly, provided you keep them well watered. What should then happen is that the roots of your chosen variety outcompete the weak rootstock which will die out, leaving you with an ungrafted tree.

Looking after your own-root tree

There is considerable variation in vigour and growth habit between different apples. This is one of the reasons why commercial orchards use rootstocks, since they allow them to have a standard size of tree for easier management. Most varieties, however, are fairly strong growers. This is great if you have a big garden and want to grow a standard tree. Don't be put off if you have a smaller garden: own-root trees can still work well, they just need more maintenance and, in particular, summer pruning. Winter pruning stimulates growth, summer pruning discourages it. Doing summer pruning as you would for a fan or espalier tree will help to keep your own-root fruit tree to a manageable size.

HOW TO PLANT A TREE

Whether you buy a tree or have raised your own, planting it into its final position always feels significant. At a time when trees could be helping to save the planet, planting a tree can become an emotional if not a political act. It's also essential that the tree not only survives but grows well and quickly. In this section we'll explore how to give your tree the best start in life so that it is still standing even when your children and grandchildren are long gone from this Earth.

Digging a hole

As a general rule, you need to dig a hole just a bit bigger than the roots of the tree you are planting. Some people recommend hole twice the size of the roots, but I have not found that to be necessary. For pot-grown trees, you can easily see how big the pot is and calculate accordingly. For bare-root plants you will need to spread out the roots to see how big the hole should be. Bare-root trees are those grown in the ground and pulled up without soil around their roots and replanted.

The hole should not be deeper than the roots, as this will leave the tree sitting too low in the soil and will risk stem rot or rooting in about the graft union. You may, however, want to fork the bottom of the hole a bit to break up heavy ground and encourage deep rooting. Check you have the depth of the hole right by laying a stick across the top of the hole and making sure the stick lines up with the right part of the tree.

If you have very heavy clay soil, there is a risk of smearing the sides of the hole as you dig. This can create a barrier to the young roots, causing them to grow around the inside of the hole rather than look for new soil. Use a garden fork to break up the sides of the hole before planting.

Preparing the roots

Bare-root trees will have little or no soil on the roots. The size of those roots will depend on the age of the tree (usually one or two years) and the vigour of the tree. For many species, you can prune the roots back before planting. Though this seems drastic, most of the small roots will already have been killed when the tree was lifted, and cutting back will encourage new growth once the tree is in the ground. In most cases I would recommend only trimming back some of the longer roots to make it easier to plant and save you having to dig an enormous hole. (Matthew Wilson, a superb commercial fruit grower from Sussex, UK, prunes his apple tree roots hard back almost to one central tap root when he plants. It makes planting much quicker and easier and has no ill effect on growth.)

Pot-grown trees are plants that have spent their life in a pot. For trees this is usually quite a large container, but still much smaller than the tree really needs. Often the roots will have started to grow around the inside of the pot – this is called being 'pot-bound'. Unless action is taken before planting, the tree roots are likely to continue to grow around in a circle in the hole after planting, meaning the tree will never thrive. In mild cases, simply take a sharp knife and cut through the thin roots around the edge. This will encourage fresh new roots that should grow outwards. In worse cases, where there are roots of pencil thickness or wider growing around the edge, use secateurs to cut through the root and tease them out of the compost a bit.

Planting

Holding the tree firmly with one hand, half fill the hole with soil, then give the tree a gentle shake to allow the soil to get in between the roots. Firm softly with your feet, then fill the rest of the hole with soil, shake again and then tread more heavily to ensure the tree is properly in the ground. If you have small children, I recommend getting them to jump up and down around the tree; otherwise, use your heel to stamp the soil into place. Pot-grown trees are easier. Just pop them in the hole, ensuring the top of the root ball lines up with the soil surface, then fill the soil around and firm in as above.

Adding compost

There are two schools of thought on this point. Historically, compost and/or fertilizer was added into the planting hole. However, more recently it is thought that this creates a lovely rich planting hole that tree roots are reluctant to leave, and that it is better to mulch on top of the tree. I subscribe to the latter, and use a mulch after planting. A good compost or woodchip mulch is in my view essential. Many growers also swear by mycorrhiza or biochar in the planting hole as part of the strategy of giving your tree the very best start.

Staking

For very tiny saplings, staking may not be necessary. The blowing wind stimulates them to grow strong roots to hold them in place. However, for anything over 60 cm (2 ft) tall I would recommend a stake, and for bigger trees a strong one is essential. It is usually easier to drive the stake in parallel to the trunk, ideally no more than 5 cm (2 in) away. With pot-grown trees, this is not always possible, in which case you can put in a diagonal stake aiming to cross the trunk at about 30 cm (12 in) from the ground (or higher for bigger trees).

There is a whole range of ties available, or you can make your own out of something soft like a pair of old tights. The key is to tie in a figure of eight, or to use a readymade spacer to ensure that the stake and the tree are not touching each other, as this will cause rubbing that can eventually break the bark and lead to disease.

It is also best practice to stake on the side of the tree that receives the most wind. The reason is that when the wind blows it won't push the tree towards the stake. This again reduces the risk of rubbing.

Watering

Though not always possible (for instance in larger woodland planting), it is a good idea to water your new tree if you can. In a dry year, or in some climates, it is essential. Watering when you plant will help to settle the soil amongst the roots ensuring good root/soil contact. The crucial period is in the tree's first spring, as the new and still shallow roots grow and look for water. In dry soils this is particularly important. I recommend watering perhaps once a week, but giving them a really good soak. Frequent, shallow watering will cause more harm than good, encouraging the roots to stay on the surface where the water is, rather than explore the lower soil levels. If watering with a hose, then leave it on a trickle next to the trunk for half an hour. You can even sink a pipe or old drinks bottle next to the trunk and water into that to ensure the water gets down below the surface. Using a good mulch will increase the water available in the soil by about 25 per cent and can be the difference between death or survival.

Mulching

Competition from weeds will have a negative impact on how well and quickly your tree grows. Here are a few options for controlling them. If you can get hold of woodchip, it is in my opinion the best option. Mulch mats can be an effective method of establishing trees, so long as you don't have voles, which will make nests underneath them. I am trying to remove any use of plastic from my growing, so would alway go for an organic mulch where possible.

If you use a compost or woodchip mulch, it needs to be at least 10 cm (4 in) thick to be effective, and make sure that it does not touch the trunk of the tree as that can result in a damp area that encourages rotting and disease.

Guards

Although less of a problem in many garden situations, you might still need to consider a guard around the trunk of the tree to prevent damage from animals such as deer, hares and rabbits that love nothing better than a winter snack of young bark. The go-to solution of recent years has been the spiral plastic guard. However, non-plastic alternatives are available. Chicken wire is good, and there are proprietary products, such as the new cactus guards, which are proving effective.

KEEPING YOUR TREE HEALTHY

You don't want to waste all the effort spent producing a beautiful and strong tree by neglecting it once it is in the ground. Sadly, many trees planted in woodland and landscaping initiatives are then abandoned to their fate with no aftercare or maintenance. The result is that survival rates can be depressingly low. Good planting with adequate mulching and watering is an essential first step, but a small effort as the tree grows pays dividends once the tree is established.

Checking tree ties

Allowing a tree to outgrow its tie is a major cause of death in urban tree planting. As the trunk gets bigger, it puts pressure on the tie, and if nothing is done the tie will eventually dig into the bark and cut off the supply of nutrients and water flowing up and down the xylem and phloem (the plant's equivalent of arteries). Using an elastic material for the tie, such as rubber, allows for some expansion, but eventually the tree will still outgrow it. Check at least once a year in early spring. If the tree still needs support, either loosen the tie or replace it with a bigger one. You may, however, find that the tree no longer needs staking and you can cut the tie off and potentially remove the stake. Eventually the stake will rot, by which time the tree should be big enough to look after itself.

Watering

Most trees in most years shouldn't need water beyond the establishment year, and indeed giving too much can be detrimental, encouraging surface rooting which is more vulnerable to drying out. However, in some circumstances extra watering will be necessary. Pot-grown trees need regular water, of course, at least once a day in really hot weather. Fruit trees grown on dwarfing rootstocks in soil may also need a drink in long, dry spells as their roots don't have the power to dig deep to find water. As with irrigating during establishment, generous infrequent watering is better than a little every day.

Pruning

Not all trees need pruning, but it can help to achieve the shape or purpose you want. In many cases some formative pruning in the first couple of years may be enough to give desired length of main stem, or encourage branching at a particular point. If you are planning to train a tree against a wall or fence then this will require ongoing pruning.

Pruning fruit trees allows you to get better-quality fruit, by allowing more light and air movement through the tree. Annual pruning can also help to balance new and older growth, the key to combating the tendency many trees have towards bienniality, when trees fruit very heavily one year and then give almost nothing the following one.

When trees grow in commercial woodlands they are planted very closely, which encourages them to grow straight, since there is little light coming from the sides. If you are trying to grow timber trees in the open, you will need to prune all side branches to give a clean, straight trunk.

Grafted trees on vigorous rootstocks can grow suckers from the base. These should be removed as soon as you see them. If left to grow, they will eventually outcompete the variety that has been grafted onto them. Don't throw it away though; if you dig up the sucker with some root attached, you can grow it as a rootstock to graft another tree onto.

Weed control

A really good mulch when planting will reduce the need to do much subsequent weeding. However, perennial weeds grow through most mulches, and for smaller trees it is sensible to keep the area around the tree weed-free for the first few years. You can do this either by additional applications of mulch, or by cutting any grass or weeds very short to avoid them competing with the tree for water and nutrients. Woodchip mulch, with an occasional flame weed, can also be an effective method. For a small number of trees, nothing beats hand weeding.

USING WOODCHIP IN YOUR GARDEN

I am a huge advocate of woodchip in the garden, and I have even written an entire book about it. Here is a quick summary of how this amazing renewable tree-based resource can benefit your garden.

Inventor Peter Jensen designed the first chipper in 1884 to deal with the prunings from the municipal parks in Maasbüll in northern Germany. Since then, chippers have mostly been used in farming and growing for two purposes: mulching paths and animal bedding. We have not fully explored or understood the potential of woodchip, and particularly the role it can play in boosting soil health and productivity.

Mulching

As I outlined on pages 68–9, a 15-cm (6-in) mulch of woodchip is a great way to give plants a good start in life. Woodchip mulch cuts out light, which will almost entirely eliminate annual weeds from your soil surface. Unlike other organic composts, fresh woodchip also prevents germination of seeds landing on it, due both to its physical nature and the allelopathic effect of the chemicals in it.

Mulches also keep water in the soil where it is useful. It does this by both shading the soil and thus lowering the temperature, and by protecting it from the wind, both of which reduce surface evaporation. Exact reductions in water loss will vary with system, mulch type, soil and climate, but are typically 25 per cent of that from an unmulched soil.

Plastic mulches give the same, if not greater, water retention, but can create an anaerobic environment underneath, which can lead to compacted and lifeless soil, and contribute nothing to the biological component of the soil.

Using a mulch of any sort can help to warm cold soils and cool hot ones. The mulch gives protection to soil and plant roots, shielding it from extremes. Most soil organisms favour temperatures of around 25°C (77°F), though fungi can cope better at cooler temperatures and bacteria at higher ones. The mulch acts as a winter coat, sunscreen lotion and umbrella combined, which helps to create better growing temperatures for both plants and soil creatures.

Bare soil is vulnerable soil. Mulching protects soil from physical damage such as heavy rain or wind, and in extreme weather conditions also helps to stop soil being washed or blown away. Woodchip mulches allow water to gently percolate through to the soil, whereas solid plastic mulches prevent the water from reaching the soil, potentially causing localized flooding issues as the rain runs off the plastic. Woodchip mulch will also prevent water from splashing on the lower leaves of a tree. This spattering in heavy rain spreads fungal spores and creates damp conditions in which the fungus can grow.

Propagation

Though composted organic material is often included in plant propagation mixes, it has not been so common to make use of woodchip for this purpose. There are commercial substrate manufacturers that use bark as the main ingredient for their products, but it is relatively easy to make your own plant-raising substrates from woodchip. Iain Tolhurst, a commercial grower in the UK, has been pioneering this technique. His homemade woodchip compost has been shown to perform just as well as a leading peat-based product.

Soil health amendment

It's hardly a news story that adding organic matter to soil is a good idea. For some reason, though, we haven't exploited woodchip for this purpose. This may be partly due to availability. Woodchip is a relatively new material; before woodchippers were invented, most woody waste would likely have been burnt. Tree surgeons now produce millions of tonnes of chip a year, and chippers are readily available to woodland managers and contractors.

Fear of nitrogen robbing, where the woodchip temporarily takes nitrogen from the soil to allow it to decompose, has also hampered using it in soil. Though there is some risk, in many cases this can be easily mitigated.

Ramial Chipped Wood (RCW) is the material you get from chipping branches less than 7 cm (2¾ in) in diameter. It has a higher proportion of nutrients (inducing nitrogen) and potentially can be spread directly onto the soil or cover crop without causing nutrient lock up. There is now a growing understanding of the role that a range of organisms, but most notably fungi, can play in improving soil health and the part that woodchip has in this process.

Looking after your tree is as important as planting it well. We don't have long to save the planet and making sure all the trees that get put in the ground actually survive is crucial. You now have the knowledge to makes sure that happens.

FORTY BEST TREES

Maple

Acer

Perhaps most famous as the symbol on the Canadian flag, the maple tree is common throughout the northern hemisphere. With its distinctive leaf shape and stunning range of autumn colours, it is popular as an ornamental tree as well as economically vital in providingthe pancake industry with maple syrup.

Good for: timber, food, wildlife

The maple's leaf is the easiest way to identify it. The shape is called palmate, which means it has lobes stemming from the leaf base. Most have between three and nine lobes. The Canadian flag shows a leaf with three lobes, while the sycamore maple

(*Acer pseudoplatanus*), which is the most common species in Europe, has five lobes. The other thing to look out for on maples is their winged seeds, also known as helicopter seeds, which spin as they fall, catching the wind to travel as far as possible from the mother tree in the hope of colonizing new ground.

The timber from larger maple species is prized for specialist items such as bowling alleys, baseball bats and furniture. The rippling grain that can occur makes some timber particularly valuable, though you usually can't tell if it will have the markings until you mill it. Maple is also great for musical instruments as it has a good mid-range resonance: drums, guitars and woodwind instruments all make use of this quality.

There are lots of maples that can be tapped for syrup and the process is relatively simple. You draw off the sap and then boil it down until enough water has evaporated to make a syrup of 67 per cent sugar. What makes the sugar maple (*Acer saccharum*) most suited is that it has particularly high levels of sugar in its sap, which means it is not necessary to boil it for so long to get to that perfect consistency. Even with sugar maple, you need 40 litres (70 pints) of sap to make 1 litre (1.75 pints) of syrup, so now you know why it is so expensive.

While some species of maple are among the most common trees on earth, many are endangered. The latest inventory showed that 36 of the total 158 species in the wild are at a high risk of extinction, with seven species being critically endangered. One of those, *Acer binzayedii*, was only discovered in 2017, a startling reminder of how quickly our biodiversity is disappearing, even before we know it is there.

Alder

Alnus

Alder is one of the world's wonder trees. It grows quickly, often in wetter soils and conditions. What makes it particularly useful is that it fixes nitrogen, helping it to establish well even in poorer soils. As a nurse crop it can shelter slower growing trees and share its nitrogen stores.

Good for: timber, medicine, wildlife, tanning, soil improvement

Alder glutinosa, also known as the black or common alder, has a few distinctive characteristics. Most typical are the purple buds in winter and similarly coloured catkins in early spring. The female parts of the flower are small fruits that look like baby cones as they mature. The big, round leaves are sometimes mistaken for the similarly shaped hazel leaves. However, alder leaves are shiny and smooth, unlike their hairy hazel counterparts.

Despite being quick growing, alder wood is very hard – very useful if you don't want it to wear out. It is also waterproof. This made it a popular choice for clog-makers (along with other wet-growing species like willow and poplar). In the mountains of Snowdonia in Wales there are still stands of alder that were originally coppiced to produce wood harvested by travelling clog makers.

Alder is what is known as a pioneer species. It can colonize bare ground quickly. This is due in large part to its symbiotic relationship with soil-living nitrogen-fixing bacteria, which pull nitrogen from the atmosphere and transform it into a soluble form that plants can take up. Red alder (*Alnus rubra*), for instance, can deliver more than 300 kg of nitrogen per hectare (1630 lb per acre) per year. This means that even if the soil is not great, the alder will grow and improve the soil making it more able to support a wider range of trees.

Alder wood, unlike that of many trees, doesn't rot in wet conditions. Indeed, the wetter the conditions in which it grows, the harder the wood will become. This is an evolutionary response that helps it to colonize areas near rivers and floodplains. It is so rot-resistant that when Venice was being built, alder was used for the pilings that held up the houses.

As a living tree, alder can also be planted to stabilize hillsides and river banks, preventing the collapse of the soil down the slope or into the river. It is thought that the Incas used it to help form their terraces which they used to grow crops on.

Banksia

Banksia

There are more than 160 species of *Banksia* ranging in size from creeping shrubs to 30 m (100 ft) tall trees. Almost all of them have a striking flower spike and subsequent cone-like fruit. They are native to Australia, where their copious production of nectar helps to feed a wide variety of wildlife, but they are now popular around the world as an ornamental plant.

Good for: wildlife, ornament, woodturning

The flower spikes of *Banksia* are most often yellow, though they also occur in a range of colours, holding thousands of individual flowers packed vertically. In one instance, 6,000 were counted on a single spike. These flower heads form distinctive cones from which the seeds emerge. The cones are often very tough and woody, to the point where they can be turned to make ornaments. Despite a lovely grain, the wood of the tree itself is not often used, as it twists when dry.

Banksia is vital to the ecology of Australia, feeding a massive assortment of creatures. Its nectar feeds birds, rodents, possums and bats and moths, while the seeds provide a protein-rich snack for cockatoos and moth larvae.

There are different species adapted to a range of soils, with a mix of sizes and growth habit. This has led to their popularity as a key garden species, while many are also cultivated for the cut flower industry. As with orchids, there are also specialist collectors breeding new cultivars and forms.

Banksia is a real survivor. There are at least nine species in New Zealand and Australia that have been around for millions of years. The most ancient pollen found was about 65 million years old. Like many Australian plants, *Banksia* is good at surviving fires. Although bush fires kill many plants, they also help to break down the protective shell of the seeds, giving them a better chance of swift germination once the fire has gone out. This enables them to grow quickly, colonizing the bare ground cleared by the fires.

Traditionally there would have been large areas of *Banksia* scrub forest in Australia, but pressures of development and land clearance for food production, as well as inappropriate fire control methods, have destroyed many of these natural habitats, leaving some species at risk of extinction. There are now programmes of protection and regeneration in place to try to help these millennia-old plants to survive.

Birch

Betula

Birch is quick-growing and, as a pioneer species, often the first tree to colonize an area of ground left untended. Its pale bark and straight stems are a striking feature in many Eastern European and Scandinavian landscapes, much used by artists for its simplicity and beauty.

Good for: timber, sap, wildlife, firewood

The birch is a relatively small tree that grows quickly when bare ground in woodland opens up. They rarely live more than 100 years, and often much less, and so are used as nurse trees for species such as oak. Reducing light at lower levels forces trees to grow straight trunks by reaching for the light higher up.

Birch timber is perfect for veneers and plywood as it splits well and is light, but still strong. Its light weight has also made it perfect for building canoes, wigwams and even skateboards.

Although maple syrup is the most famous tree sap product, birch is also perfect for tapping (the name given to collecting tree sap as it rises in the early spring). Cut a small branch or drill a hole in the bark and the pressure from the roots pushing sap into the growing tree will force it out into your collection bucket. In a good year on a big tree, you might get 5 litres (8.75 pints) of sap. You can drink it fresh or make wine or syrup from it.

The Hughes Aircraft Company designed and built the largest flying boat out of wood during the Second World War, since aluminium was in short supply. Despite its unkind nickname of the 'Spruce Goose', the plane was actually made mostly of birch, and took so long to build it was too late to see any action and made only one short flight in 1947. You can still see it at the Evergreen Aviation Museum in Oregon.

If you are interested in music quality, then look out for speakers made of birch wood, which has unusual resonance features. The structure of wood has an impact on how it reacts to soundwaves, and birch resonates well at both high and low frequencies, giving music more clarity, though less volume than woods like maple, which have a greater mid-range resonance.

In the days before sticking plasters, birch bark was peeled off and placed on minor wounds. It gives some physical protection but the chemicals present in the bark also stimulate tissue healing.

Bottle Brush

Callistemon

The striking and brightly coloured flowers that are shaped in a long cylinder are what gives this tree the common name of bottlebrush. *Callistemon* is native to Australia, but the trees' beauty and ease of cultivation has led them to be adopted around the world, despite not being entirely frost hardy.

Good for: ornament, leaves/flowers used as tea, wildlife

The bright, red flower spikes attract a whole host of creatures, including bees and other insects, hummingbirds and other honey eaters that feed on their bounty of nectar. Many species also produce seeds that provide food for birds that prefer something with a bit of crunch.

Callistemon has a great survival strategy that it evolved in the harsh Australian environment; it grows its seeds in little fruiting capsules on its stems. They are pretty hard to get into, which is why specialist birds like rosellas with strong beaks do better on them. They don't release their seed every year, which means that bottlebrush can give a long-term food supply. Some species won't let go of their seed until there is fire – a great way to take advantage of the lack of competition from other plants after a forest fire.

The leaves and flowers are used as tea, and have a fresh almondy taste.

In 1977, a Californian researcher noticed that it was really hard to get plants to survive near the lemon bottlebrush (*Callistemon citrinus*). On closer inspection, he found that the soil surrounding the plants had very high levels of a chemical called leptospermone, which has an allelopathic effect on other plants. Allelopathy is the name given to the negative impact, usually on growth or germination, that one plant can cause to others through the release of natural chemicals. He then tested the effect of the isolated leptospermone on plant growth and found that it could be used to kill them. However, it didn't kill maize, which seems to have an in-built resistance to the chemical. This led to the development of Mesotrione, a herbicide which can be sprayed on the soil before the maize germinates, killing off the other weeds but allowing the maize to grow through. It is interesting to see how these chemicals are often developed by mimicking what is happening in nature, even though we then employ them in a way that destroys that very nature that inspired them.

Chestnut

Castanea

Chestnuts have delicious, nutritious nuts and hard-wearing, straight-growing timber. With these qualities it's no wonder that humans have had a long close relationship with them. Sometimes, however, being the favourite child is not always good for you, as we shall see.

Good for: timber, nuts, wildlife, tanning

We have been eating chestnuts for a long time. They are mentioned by writers such as Xenophon, Theophrastus and Pliny, and the Greeks are credited with taking chestnuts to Italy as they migrated across the Ionian and Adriatic seas. Unlike many other nuts, chestnuts are not that high in protein, but do provide a useful form of carbohydrate, making them a potential alternative source of energy for humans. Growing a millable crop from trees, rather than having to cultivate annual crops like wheat and rye, could have an impact on climate change. You can also add chestnuts to livestock feed, and many animals will browse on the leaves.

The high tannin content was also exploited to tan leather in the days before synthetic tannins became the norm. As well as dyeing the hides a dark brown, chestnut produces flexible waterproof leather particularly suited to making shoes.

Historically, chestnut has been coppiced to make fence posts and shingles. The wood doesn't rot quickly when left outside, or

sunk into the ground. A fifteen-to-twenty-year coppicing cycle should supply a good-sized straight growth for fence posts.

We don't have a great record as a species for understanding the complex interconnectedness of nature. We look for simple solutions to complicated challenges. For example, we imported small Chinese chestnuts into America as the native ones were so big it was harder to harvest them commercially. Unfortunately, these Asian trees brought in a new disease that they were mostly resistant to, but which native species were unable to cope with. The result was the near-extinction of the American chestnut. This is a mistake we have made again and again. However, there is hope, as new resistant trees are now being bred. We have learned something from the experience with American chestnuts and the approach now is not to remove all trees as soon as disease shows, but to see whether any trees survive and look for natural resistance to new diseases among native populations of trees.

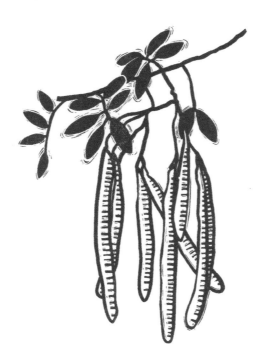

Indian Bean Tree

Catalpa

In spite of its common name, *Catalpa* is neither a member of
the legume family nor from India. However, the fruit is a long,
thin bean shape, up to 50 cm (20 in) long, which hangs down from
the branches, making it a very distinctive ornamental tree.

Good for: timber, wildlife, medicine

Catalpa is a versatile timber; it is resistant to rotting so is often
used for fence posts. Since it is not especially hard, it can be
easily worked, so it is commonly used in furniture making and
woodturning for ornamental features that might be difficult to
create from harder woods.

   Catalpa has huge, luxurious, flat, pointed leaves, bigger than a human hand, thought to attract wildlife keen to hide out and shelter from the rain. This also makes it a great tree to grow near your outdoor sitting area. It comes into leaf late in the spring, allowing you to make the most of the early-season sun, but providing useful summer shade as the weather gets hotter and the sun higher.

If mega-long fruit and big leaves weren't enough, *Catalpa* also has showy flowers, usually white or yellowish, with a similar shape and appearance to orchid flowers.

How did the Indian bean get its name if it is not from India? Some species are native to North America and the fruits are said to be hallucinogenic when smoked. As this pastime was attributed to some Native American tribes, the tree was called 'Indian', or the cigar tree for the same reason.

Not many trees are planted for their usefulness to fishing, but *Catalpa* is host to a caterpillar of the catalpa sphinx moth (*Ceratomia catalpae*), also called the catalpa worm, which is highly prized as bait for certain fish. If left unchecked, the worm can strip the tree of its soft leaves, but there are parasitic flies and wasps that usually keep it under control. In some areas, keen fishermen plant the tree just to have ready access to the worm.

The root of the tree is poisonous, but over the centuries other parts of the tree have been used to treat a wide range of ailments, from snake bites to asthma. Tea made from the bark also has sedative properties, and the quinine in it made it useful in reducing malaria parasite numbers in the blood.

Cedar

Cedrus

Cedar is a group of evergreen trees originating in the mountains of the Himalayas and the Mediterranean. Their magnificent form made them a favourite of the grand estates of England, and they are now grown from Australia to the Americas as an ornamental tree.

Good for: timber, ornamental moth repellent

There are a wider range of trees from other genera that are called cedars, such as the white cedar and western red cedar, but I shall concentrate here on *Cedrus*. As older trees, cedars are mostly recognizable by their needles held in clusters and their growth habit, which tends towards a thick trunk with horizontal spreading branches. The length of these heavy branches make them vulnerable to breaking, so in veteran trees you often see a very thick trunk with uneven limbs. But like oak trees they can survive this damage to reach a ripe old age. The Koca Katran Lebanon Cedar in Turkey is estimated to be more than 2,000 years old.

Most cedars are large and regularly reach 50 m (160 ft) in height. Their vertically held, barrel-shaped cones are also distinctive, sometimes a purplish grey or blue, turning to reddish brown as they mature in autumn.

The oils in cedars are highly repugnant to insects and in particular to the moth that eats clothes. For this reason chests and wardrobes are often made from its wood, and small cubes of the wood are sold for placing among our precious garments. In Homer's *Iliad*, the treasure chamber used by King Priam of Troy is described as lined with cedar wood.

In ancient Egypt, the preservative qualities of cedar wood were tapped, with the resin and sawdust being used as part of the mummification process. The antimicrobial resin was rubbed onto the dead body to slow down its decomposition. According to Herodotus, it was possibly even injected into the intestines. The sawdust, meanwhile, would be packed into the abdominal cavity.

Not surprisingly, given its geographical origin, the Lebanon cedar tree features prominently in both the Quran and the Bible. In the former it marks, covered with angels, the boundary beyond which stands Paradise. In the Bible, Solomon is said to have built Jerusalem from the timber of cedar and fir. Its height and strength were bywords for power and longevity.

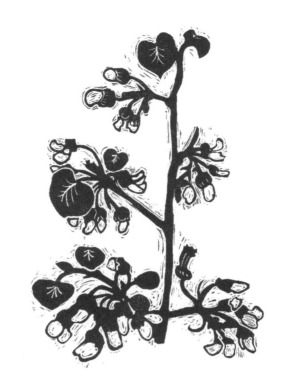

Redbud

Cercis

Cercis is a group of small leguminous trees and shrubs that have the
most amazing display of edible pinkish-purple flowers that come
out before the leaves in early spring. The fat buds that precede this
exhibition are fat and red, giving it its common name of redbud.

Good for: food, dyes, timber, wildlife

The timber is soft and not suitable for construction, but
has interesting grains, so it has been used for veneers and
woodturning. Like many leguminous plants, however, it does
give us something to eat. The flowers can be eaten raw in salads.

If you can't wait for them to come out, you can pick the buds and pickle them. The seed pods and seeds can be eaten, too. Even the green twigs at the ends of the branches can be used as a spice to season stews and meat. This is so widespread that the tree has the alternative name of spicewood tree.

The early flowers are a great source of nectar for wildlife. They have a deep flower, so attract animals that can get all the way down, such as hummingbirds and carpenter bees. The seeds, meanwhile, provide food for a range of birds and even squirrels. There are also at least nineteen species of caterpillar that have been observed eating the leaves.

The most famous species of *Cercis* is the Judas tree (*C. siliquastrum*). Some say that the tree got its name from being the tree that Judas hung himself from after his betrayal of Jesus. You can see it might fit the bill, since it grows in the right region, and has a horizontal growth habit that would provide ample branches at about the right height to attach a noose. Despite this negative connotation, its value as an early spring show has ensured its popularity in our gardens.

George Washington wrote in his diary about the many hours he spent propagating seedlings of the *Cercis* that he had gathered from wild trees in his local forests. In the same way that Jefferson had an affection for dogwood, Washington had his finger on the pulse with his admiration for the eastern redbud, which later became the state tree for Oklahoma. There is a story that it nearly didn't get chosen because of its association with Judas, and the Church had to reassure the state authorities that redbud was not mentioned in the Bible.

Dogwood

Cornus

With a range of brightly coloured barks, these trees are
mostly grown for ornamental purposes now, and are a
mainstay in municipal designs. They are hardy and give
winter colour in what might otherwise be drab and empty
urban planting. Many have lovely flowers and the
seeds and fruit of most species are edible.

Good for: fruit, timber, wildlife, ornament

Exactly how *Cornus* got its common name of dogwood is not
verified but one theory is that it came from 'dagwood', as the thin
wood is really hard and was used to make daggers and skewers.

When I did my horticultural training, we learned to distinguish
bare *Cornus* winter twigs from similar willow branches by the
oppositely arranged buds. There are a great range of vibrant
red- and green-coloured varieties, including C. 'Midwinter Fire',
which looks almost as if the bushes are ablaze.

Dogwoods support a wide range of wildlife; birds eat the fruits
and nest in their dense branches, while insects are attracted by
the flowers. The gray dogwood (*C. racemosa*) is the main host
for azure butterflies (*Celastrina ladon*), who lay their eggs on the
flower buds.

The tree is the state flower of both North Carolina and
Virginia. Virginia is also the only state to have the same symbolic
flower and tree, so they must really love dogwood.

In times gone, by before Tinder and Grindr, women were sent dogwood flowers as a token of affection. Rather than swiping left or right, the woman would either keep the flowers to show she was keen, or send them back. For experts who understood the subtlety, there were even different types of affection: white meant pure nonsexual love, while pink showed amorous intent.

As with many trees, there are legends about the dogwood and Christ. In one story, the Cross was made from *Cornus*, which the myth says, used to be a big tree. The dogwood was so upset by its role in the crucifixion that God allowed it to grow small and so never again to be able to be used for that purpose. The shape of the bracts form a cross in remembrance of this. A bract is a modified leaf that often surrounds a flower and in some plants can be more striking than the flower itself.

Hazel

Corylus

Hazel is especially versatile and all the more useful for not growing into a massive tree. It can be grown as a specimen even in modest gardens, producing delicious nuts, though saving them from being scoffed by squirrels in the UK is always a challenge. Hazel is perfectly suited to coppicing, with new shoots growing very straight from the base.

Good for: nuts, timber, wildlife

Hazel has big, flat, soft, hairy leaves, with a smooth brownish-grey bark. The catkins, which are the male flowers, are a striking characteristic and, if tapped at the right time, will produce a cloud of pollen. By contrast, the female flowers are tiny and red, almost invisible. Both male and female flowers are found on the same tree (this is called monoecious).

Left to grow unpruned, the hazel has a typical tree shape that a child might draw. When coppiced, however, it produces a more compact bush. How often to coppice depends on what you want to produce and how good your soil is. Five-year cutting is normally the minimum for making hurdles and bean poles. If growing for firewood, a 10–15-year cycle is more suitable. Coppiced hazel is also great for wildlife, providing shorter understory in mixed woodlands, and is an especially good habitat for the dormouse. Young coppiced growth is used for fencing hurdles, walking sticks, thatching spars and bean poles. Thicker timber is used for woodfuel.

Hazelnuts are a staple crop for many countries and likely to become more common as a protein alternative to meat in our diets. Southern Europe and the Middle East have typically been the main hazelnut producers, though they grow well in more northern climates too.

Hazel was one of the woods used traditionally by water diviners, with its combination of strength and flexibility. In Celtic mythology, hazel also has a strong association with water, with nine hazel trees supposedly growing around the well of wisdom. In Norse mythology, the hazel is associated with wisdom.

In the 1860s a contorted form of hazel was found, probably in a hedge, in Tortworth, south Gloucestershire in the west of England, just 32 km (20 miles) from where I live. This tree was the origin of all the specimens of contorted hazel grown around the world, which are mostly now grafted onto a straight plant for added vigour. We have one in our garden, and named our dog after it.

Hawthorn

Crataegus

The hawthorn is a large group of shrubs and small
trees usually with red berries. A key species in creating
livestock-proof fencing, its name comes from the
Old English word *haw*, meaning hedge. The clouds of
white blossom that emerge in late spring have led to
it also being called mayflower.

Good for: medicine, wildlife, hedging, ornament

There are many hundreds of species of *Crataegus* originating
in much of the northern hemisphere. It has sharp thorns and
responds well to pruning, so was used extensively in creating
boundaries for domesticated animals. Thorn apple, quickthorn
and whitethorn are some of its other common names that
celebrate the tree's spikes. In most species, red fruit develops in
mid-autumn but it can stay on the trees well into winter.

The hawthorn can support more than 300 insects, including
some species like the hawthorn ermine moth (*Yponomeuta
padella*) that rely on it as a host. Dormice feed off its flowers,
while a huge range of birds and other mammals eat the fruit. Its
thorny branches provide a safe nesting place too.

The fruit of the Chinese hawthorn (*Crataegus pinnatifida*)
is larger and widely harvested for food. The berries of other
species are mostly very small and can take a long time to pick
in sufficient quantities, though they have traditionally been

made into jelly or wine. Hawthorn has some useful medicinal properties, too, particularly for digestive disorders.

In many cultures, hawthorn trees were believed to ward off evil spirits and sorcery. The flowers herald the start of true spring and new hope. In Slavic folklore, to successfully kill a vampire you had to use a hawthorn stake. A whole raft of superstitions grew up around the tree to prevent the dead rising as vampires, such as scattering hawthorn twigs at the funeral, or even putting stakes into the graves of the dead so that if they did turn into a vampire they would impale themselves before they could come and get you.

'Ne'er cast a clout till may be out.' This old saying gives some guidance on when to stop wearing your winter coat in case you pack it away too soon and regret your impatience. The true sign that summer is on its way is not the end of the month of May, but rather the mayflower coming into bloom.

Handkerchief tree

Davidia involucrata

Unlike some genera of plants that have hundreds of species, *Davidia* has only this one. It is most famous for its large, white bracts that resemble white handkerchiefs or doves dancing in the wind. Originating in China, it is now grown as an ornamental throughout the world.

Good for: ornament

Growing up to 25 m (80 ft) in height, *Davidia* has linden-like leaves and small, maroon flowerheads, overshadowed by the large white bracts that give this tree its many common names.

Exploration and trade have played a huge part in the spread of plants and *Davidia* is no exception. It all started in the late 1860s with a French priest called Armand David. David was a typical nineteenth-century polymath, and on one of his zoological and botanical explorations found a *Davidia* specimen high up in the mountains of China. Dried flowers and leaves from this specimen joined the hundreds of other plants and animals he brought back to Paris, to the delight of the French government and public. He was also responsible for bringing back the less delightful emerald ash borer (*Agrilus planipennis*), a beetle that has gone on to be a serious pest in many countries.

The French material became well known, and others went in search of the tree in the hope of getting seeds to propagate. Augustine Henry, an amateur plant hunter and medical officer from Scotland, had somehow got hold of a map, though not a very detailed one, with a large X on it, in pirate style, marking the location of the tree. However, Augustine was being sent home and so passed on this scrap of a clue to Ernest Wilson, who had been commissioned by Kew Gardens in London to go plant-hunting. He was only twenty-two, spoke no Chinese and had to fight through hostile territory in a time of significant anti-European feeling, but despite all of this he managed to find the tree that Armand had chanced upon thirty years before, only to discover that it had been recently cut down to build a house. After 21,000 km (13,000 miles) of struggle, he must have been devastated to see just a stump remaining. Fortunately, on his way home he found a grove of the trees growing in a gorge and was able to collect seed, which he brought back to England.

Gum tree

Eucalyptus

Though rightly famous for feeding koalas, and for the aroma of the oils produced in its leaves, the gum tree is much more than just a decongestant, cuddly animal food. It grows very quickly and is resistant to most pests and so has been key to the timber and paper industry. However, climate change is threatening its success as high temperatures slow down the growth of many species in its native Australia.

Good for: timber, medicinal, ornamental, wildlife

There are more than 700 species of *Eucalyptus* and they've been around for at least 35 million years. Though height and growth habits vary, they all have tough waxy leaves that release their characteristic minty smell if you rub them. Many species change their leaf shape between young and mature growth. The young leaves are a staple of flower bouquets as they provide long-lasting green structure to the arrangements.

Didgeridoos, reputedly the world's oldest instrument, are made from eucalyptus branches that have been hollowed out by termites, who eat the softer wood inside, leaving the harder outside shell.

Eucalyptus wood has very short and even fibres, which make it perfect for making high-quality paper. It is also suitable for charcoal making and bioenergy. There are huge plantations in many parts of the world, particularly in the Americas. As you might expect, large-scale planting of non-native species is not always popular, and runs the risk of displacing the local flora and fauna. Interestingly, however, a study done in California found that the diversity of species supported by *Eucalyptus* was similar to native trees, though the species were different.

The high levels of volatile oils in *Eucalyptus* can be dangerous. They are so flammable that forest fires spread quickly through their branches and in some cases the trees even explode, but they have also evolved to recover from fire. Their growth buds are protected under the bark and once the danger of fire has passed, they will quickly regrow.

If you are looking to get into gold mining, then *Eucalyptus* could be your friend. Trees growing above gold deposits have been found to have tiny particles of gold in their leaves. While you won't get enough gold from the tree itself to make it worth the effort of processing, they could help show where it is worth digging down to find the precious metal.

Spindle

Euonymus

Euonymus is a group of trees, shrubs and climbing plants, most notable for their brightly coloured fruit. Variegated forms are a popular ornamental shrub; tough and evergreen, they are a common choice for urban landscapers. In the UK, the appearance of spindles is an indicator you might be in ancient woodland.

Good for: timber, wildlife, medicine

The leaves and flowers are similar to dogwood, but once the fruits form there is no mistaking the spindle tree. The brilliant pink or white popcorn-like fruits surround orange or red seeds. At a time of year when most trees are dying, this splash of colour is a real joy. The unusual colour of some *Euonymus* species has led to a wide variety of common names: strawberry bush, wahoo and burning bush (*E. alatus*, which is considered invasive in parts of America), to name a few.

The name spindle comes from the fact that the hard dense wood was perfectly suited to making spindles for spinning, as well as pegs and butchers' skewers. It's a great choice for artists' charcoal too, because the close grain and durability prevent it from breaking easily.

Spindle fruit provides a useful late food source for wildlife. Birds in particular seem to be immune to the toxicity that affects humans, and the robin is especially fond of the coloured snack. Mice and even foxes are also able to eat it. The tree also supports many moths and other insects.

In the fairy tale of 'Sleeping Beauty' I was always confused by the fact that she pricked her finger on the spindle of the spinning wheel, which is not sharp. But in earlier versions of the story it is the spindle tree she pricks herself on, which makes a little more sense, particularly since the berries and seeds are poisonous to humans and in extreme cases can cause hallucinations and unconsciousness. Diarrhoea and sickness are more common symptoms, and it is worth warning children not to eat the berries, however much they look like tempting sweets.

Despite these risks, some parts of the plant are reputed to have beneficial effects when used carefully. The bark has been used to treat liver problems, while the ground-up fruit and seeds are effective against lice if you rub them on your head. Don't try this without professional advice, though, since allergic reactions to the plant are common.

Beech

Fagus

Beech trees are one of the dominant hardwood trees in
Northern Europe, with other species throughout North
America and Asia. Unusual for a deciduous tree, it keeps its
brown leaves through autumn and into winter. I've always
had a soft spot for the copper beech, since we had a splendid
specimen next door to one of my childhood homes.

Good for: timber, woodfuel, nuts, wildlife

Beech is one of the larger trees in most landscapes, sometimes
called the mother or queen of the woods, growing up to 40 m
(130 ft) tall. It can also be identified in winter by its brownish-
red, pointed leaf buds. The leaves have a rich, shiny texture.

Beech is particularly good for firewood, which no doubt is one
reason for its popularity historically. It can also be used for rough
building work and furniture, but it is not very stable, so tends
not to be used for finer or decorative work. It's a key part of
flavouring many smoked foods and alcoholic drinks.

Beech is also commonly used as a hedging plant. It responds
well to pruning, so you can shape it for ornamental purposes
and, since it hangs on to its dead leaves, it provideds visual
protection in winter. The tallest hedge in the world, and the
longest in Britain, is the Meikleour Beech Hedge in Scotland,
measured by the Guinness Book of Records at 30 m (98 ft) tall
and 530 m (1,740 feet) long.

Beech trees arrived in the UK 4,000 years ago, perhaps brought by Neolithic tribes to grow for their edible nuts, which, although small and a little bitter, are highly nutritious. They are particularly attractive to squirrels, as is the young wood of the tree, which has made establishing new planting of beech trees in the UK, where grey squirrels are now dominant, very tricky indeed.

Carving your initials into the bark of a tree is something many of us will have done as children, though not something to be encouraged, since it can damage the tree. This tree graffitti (also known as 'arborglyphs') actually has a long history going back many centuries, with some populations carving spiritual or memorial images or words into the bark. Beeches, along with other pale-coloured trees, were chosen as they can preserve the scratchings even many years after they were drawn.

Fig
Ficus

There are more than 800 species of *Ficus*, most of which produce edible fruit, though only a very small number are cultivated commercially. *F. carica* is the main fruit species, but historically *F. elastica* was used for rubber production. While *F. benjamina* (always a favourite, as it bears my name) is a popular house plant.

Good for: fruit, rubber, ornament, wildlife

Though the shape varies according to species, fig leaves tend to be shiny and often large, which is presumably what made them Adam and Eve's go-to choice of underwear in the Garden of Eden. The fruit of *F. carica* has green or purple skin, and juicy, red flesh full of tiny seeds, which if you time it right explodes in your mouth, and probably dribbles juice down your chin. Figs are native to the Mediterranean, and most commercial production is still in that area, though they are now grown around the world and, given some protection (and ideally a sunny wall to grow against), it can survive even in relatively cold conditions.

Latex is the milky excretion that many plants give off when they are cut. In a few species the volume and chemical composition of this latex makes it viable to process it into products. *Ficus elastica* was the most widely used source of latex for the rubber industry until it was replaced in the early twentieth century by *Hevea brasiliensis*, a higher-yielding but unrelated tree.

Fig pollination is one of the most extraordinary stories of co-evolution. Almost every species of fig has a specific wasp (or small number of species) that pollinate them. This is how it works: a female wasp burrows into a male fruit and lays her eggs, which hatch and mate with each other. The males have one final job to do before ending their short life, which is to eat an escape tunnel out of the fruit for the females, who then fly off, covered in pollen. The female wasps then have to find a female fruit, which they crawl into, losing their wings and antennae as they creep in. The pollen fertilizes this female fruit and the wasp dies inside the fruit. Don't panic though: the fig has an enzyme, ficain, which breaks down the wasp body before we eat the fruit.

Ash

Fraxinus

Ash is a cornerstone tree in the Northern Hemisphere, with a range of medium-to-large species. In Europe we are currently experiencing the devastating effects of ash dieback disease, a fungal disease that is spreading rapidly, not helped by the global trade in tree seedlings without sufficient health checks.

Good for: timber, firewood, wildlife, livestock browse

The common name (from the Old English æsċ) and the Latin name *Fraxinus* both mean 'spear', as the wood was often used to make the shaft. It combines strength with some flexibility. Odin and Thor were both said to have spears made from ash. These qualities have also shaped how it is used as timber – for instance, as staircases, bows and carriage frames. Some models of the Morgan sports car, such as the SP1, still use ash in their frames.

Ash is known as the king of firewood; it produces a clean, long-lasting heat, but is also one of the few woods that can be successfully burnt green (that is, without seasoning or drying). The tree also coppices well, so is suited for managing as a continuously cropped tree for woodfuel.

Yggdrasil, or the Viking 'World Tree', was an ash, its trunk stretching up into the skies, the roots down to the underworld, while its branches extended across the earthly realms. The tree hosted many mythical creatures, such as Ratatoskr the squirrel, reflecting the reality of the tree's benefit to wildlife.

In North America, native ash trees are particularly low in tannins, which make them a valuable source of food and habitat for native frog species. However, these low tannin levels also make it rather tasty to the ash leaf borer (*Agrilus planipennis*), and as borer populations have increased, other species with higher tannin levels are becoming more dominant. This is, of course, good news for overall tree health and numbers but not so good for the poor frogs, which are now under threat.

There's a saying in the UK: 'Ash before oak, in for a soak; oak before ash, just a splash.' Whichever tree comes into leaf first will determine how wet the spring will be. Both sprout at the same time, and the reason for variation over different years is that oak responds mainly to temperature, while the ash's leaves are determined more by daylight. So an early warm spring will encourage the oak, while ash will win in a colder year. There is no evidence that the latter actually results in more rain, however.

Honey locust

Gleditsia triacanthos

Described by some as an aggressive and invasive tree, *Gleditsia* is a quick grower with huge thorns. It is able to quickly colonize new areas, allowing it to outcompete slower-growing species. It has become a major pest in some areas of the world, but properly managed has much to offer.

Good for: timber, food

Honey locust has a delicate frondy foliage that contrasts with its vicious thorns. It comes into leaf relatively late in spring, making it a popular ornamental plant when winter shading is an issue.

The flowers hang in cream-coloured clusters and have a strong, heady aroma. Less-invasive varieties have been bred for those wanting to include in gardens and parks, but it's suckering nature can still make it tricky to contain.

Gleditsia timber is very hard and gives a good grain, so it has been used for furniture. Its most common use, however, is probably for fence posts, since it coppices well, giving multiple straight trunks that are tough and resistant to rot. In the days before iron, the 15 cm (6 in) steely thorns would be used as nails.

Like other members of the legume family (*Fabaceae*), the honey locust produces pods and seeds that are highly nutritious. They are edible to humans, for instance ground up as a coffee substitute, while the pulp of the pods can be eaten raw or even processed into sugar. The high protein levels in the seeds and pods also make it an ideal alternative to annually grown animal-feed crops like soya. For livestock that like to browse, the leaves are also tasty and nutritious.

The common name of this tree is rather confusing. It seemingly has little to do with either bees or locusts, though the flowers do provide some food for the former. The honey bit of its name comes from the sweet pod pulp, which was widely eaten in its native North America. The locust part (which it shares with other related species like the black locust and water locust trees) is derived from the appearance of the pods. It is thought that when John the Baptist went out into the desert and survived on honey and locusts, he was not in fact munching on insects but harvesting the pods of the carob tree, which is a relative of the *Gleditsia*.

Holly

Ilex

For many of us, Holly is synonymous with Christmas,
the shiny evergreen leaves and bright red berries bringing
a touch of the woods into our winter celebrations.
It has long been a source of winter shelter and browse
for livestock, and the pale, fine-grained wood is superb
for walking sticks and furniture making.

Good for: timber, decoration, wildlife, livestock feed

There are over 560 species of holly, of extremely diverse sizes and habits. Some are trees, others shrubs and there are even some climbing types. *Ilex aquifolia* is the most well known and the one normally used for decorations at Christmas. The leaves are a lustrous deep green with sharp, pointed lobes. These leafy spikes are a defence mechanism evolved to protect against browsing. However, since animals like deer can only reach so high, the plant did not need to protect its higher branches, meaning many species have smooth leaves on their upper limbs, which we don't often see at ground level. Lots of animals have co-evolved to cope with the spiny deterrent, and will happily munch through the sharp leaves.

Holly is dioecious. This means that it has separate male and female plants. This is why you see berries on some trees and not on others. If you are planting hollies in an area where there aren't any others, plant both sexes to ensure a supply of berries.

Holly's symbolic importance predates Christmas. Ancient pagans decorated their houses with it to celebrate the Winter Solstice, when it was a symbol of hope and new growth. In ancient Rome, too, the holly was sacred, linked to the god Saturn. Like so many older rituals, it was adopted into Christian practice, with the red berries signifying the blood of Christ. In the UK, holly was one of the species used as a Christmas tree before Queen Victoria popularized the use of yew.

Although Hollywood was not, in fact, named after the holly tree, commercial holly woods were planted in the UK. Large quantities were used for making the groynes used in protecting beaches against coastal erosion. There is also a nineteenth-century record of 150,000 trees being felled to supply the cotton mills in the north-west of England with bobbins. Large-scale plantings of holly are not common, however, and the tree is usually found as part of mixed woodlands.

Walnut

Juglans

As someone who likes bitter foods, I love the sour tang of the walnut and eat more than my fair share of the roughly 2 million tons consumed every year worldwide. The trees have a beautiful spreading shape, too, and wonderfully large leaves, which make it a great ornamental tree.

Good for: timber, nuts, wildlife

The walnut is most commonly grown for nuts or timber, with different species grown for each purpose. Though mostly picked ripe and shelled, most species can be harvested when young and either pickled in vinegar or preserved in sugar. Oil, liquors and other specialty products and dishes have helped to cement walnuts into the heart of many cultures. I highly recommend

Roger Deakin's book *Wildwood: A Journey through Trees* for its passages exploring the walnut forests of Kyrgyzstan.

Walnut wood has also been prized over the millennia. It has dense beautiful graining that polishes well, and is very hard-wearing, perfect for furniture as well as being the wood of choice for gun makers. The beautiful markings have led it to be used for veneers, with the burrs being particularly sought after. Burrs (or burls) occur where the wood grows around a foreign body – usually a fungal infection or something that has lodged into the wood, creating a wonderful pattern in the timber.

Walnuts contain a superpower in the form of the chemical juglone, which can be toxic to a range of plants and animals. It has an allelopathic effect on nearby plants, preventing seeds from germinating or plants from growing. This presumably is an evolutionary device which allows it to maximize available resources rather than having to share them with competitors. Some plants are more susceptible than others to its effects. The leaves and bark can also poison animals, though they will normally only eat it if they are not being fed a well balanced and healthy diet. The juglone is broken down by the composting process, however, so if you have woodchip containing walnuts it is safe to use after about three months.

Walnuts are one of the few nuts that can be extracted leaving the shell intact in two halves. There are numerous fairy tales that incorporate walnuts or walnut shells into the narrative. For instance, Thumbelina slept in a polished walnut shell, while the Brothers Grimm often recounted tales of dresses or magical creatures hidden inside walnut shells until they were needed.

Magnolia

Magnolia

Considered by many to be the first flowering tree ever to have existed, the magnolia has been living on the earth before bees evolved. Notable for very early and splashy flowers, many species bloom before the leaves come out in spring. They are a popular ornamental plant around the world.

Good for: timber, medicine, food, ornament

I am particularly fond of magnolias, partly because we had a huge one growing in our garden when I was young, but also there is a fine collection in the botanic gardens of my native city of Bath. I always try to get there in early spring, since some species are among the very first trees and shrubs to come into bloom. Their large flamboyant, scented flowers are pollinated by beetles, who bumble around between the tough stamens in search of sweet nectar. Later in the year, magnolias form distinctive cone-shaped fruit or seed pods. These can be dried and used for decoration. The flowers and buds are edible, and so large they can provide a significant snack. *Magnolia grandiflora* petals have a spicy taste when pickled, while buds can be used for tea or for even steamed as a vegetable.

The plant is most commonly grown as an ornamental garden tree or shrub, and a large hybridization industry has spread as growers look for new forms to tempt us.

As perhaps the oldest tree to form flowers, the magnolia was too early to develop complicated and specialist pollination strategies with specific butterfly or bee species. Instead it evolved to make use of the insects that were about at the time, which were mostly flies and flightless beetles. These are rather unkindly known as 'dumb pollinators', since they have no complicated relationships with their symbiotic plants. The flower structure is relatively simple and pollinators just get dusted in pollen as they wander between flowers feeding on nectar and eating the tasty flower parts.

The magnolia is the state flower of Mississippi, and features on its new state flag. The previous version, which incorporated the Confedrate flag in its design, was dropped in 2020 as a result of intense public pressure following civil rights protests. The flower represents hope and rebirth, particularly since the magnolia will often flower more than once in a season, and stays in bloom for a long time.

Apple
Malus

Originating from central Asia, the apple is perhaps the most widely cultivated fruit in the world. It grows in a variety of climates, stores well and makes delicious juice and alcoholic drinks. There are at least 7,500 known cultivars, though there are likely to be many more grown by chance from discarded pips.

Good for: fruit, timber, wildlife

The apple is a member of the rose family and the blossom is not unlike a small version of a wild rose. Growing on their own roots, apple trees can grow up to 5 m (16 ft) tall, depending on the

variety, but most trees nowadays are grafted onto a rootstock to give a tree of a predictable size or to benefit from the disease-resistant genetics of the rootstock.

Apple wood has good, dense grain and has been used for tool handles and musical instruments. Chipped applewood is used for smoking and flavouring food.

I come from the South West of England, where there is a rich history of fruit cultivation and breeding. Leafing through the names of old fruit varieties is a real joy. Some are named after their place of origin, many of which I am familiar with. However, there is also a rich vein of humorous variety names, some of which seem to have been thought up when under the influence of cider made from the fruit, such as 'Dog's Snout', 'Hen's Turds' and 'Slack-ma-Girdle'.

'Beauty of Bath', named after my home town, is one of the earliest to fruit, but must be eaten almost immediately. Very late varieties such as 'Christmas Pippin' (found growing by a road in Somerset, England) or 'Cornish Gilliflower' are picked even into early winter.

Any variety can be fermented to make an alcoholic cider, though many dessert apples are too sweet to produce an interesting drink, so more acidic cider varieties have been bred. In cider-producing areas of the UK, workers were often paid part of their wages in cider, popular in a time when drinking water might not always have been safe. However, I imagine that worker productivity dropped off towards the end of the day as the intake of the intoxicating tipple took effect.

Redwood

Metasequoia, Sequoia, Sequoiadendron

Redwood is the common name given mainly to a group of three genera: *Metasequoia*, *Sequoia* and *Sequoiadendron*. The tallest, biggest and longest-living trees in the world are redwoods. They are also survivors, known to have been alive in the Jurassic period, about 200 million years ago.

Good for: timber

These trees really are giants. It is not unusual to see coastal redwood trees (*Sequoia sempervirens*) over 90 m (300 ft) tall, with the record currently being held by the Hyperion Tree in the Redwood National Park in California, clocking in at 116 m (380 ft). The coastal redwood is a particularly valuable timber, prized for being very resistant to rotting, and strong but light.

Native to China, *Metasequoia* is one of the few deciduous conifer trees (larch being the most notable other one). They are also smaller than many other redwoods. This combination has made them popular ornamental trees in cities, allowing light in winter and shade in summer.

The *Sequoidendrum* has perhaps my favourite of all common names: 'big tree'. If you crush the foliage it will smell of aniseed. The cones can stay on the tree with viable seed for as long as thirty years, often needing a forest fire to stimulate their release.

Unlike many conifers, its bark doesn't have resin. While you might think that would make it less durable, it allows the wood to

absorb water, making it less likely to catch fire. Timber-framed houses clad in redwood that were caught in the San Francisco fires of 1906 tended to survive. It is thought that without them the fire would have spread much further.

Sequoias are so big that in previous centuries, some – such as the Chandelier Tree in Leggett, California – have been hollowed out to form an arch to walk or drive through. However, this not surprisingly causes significant damage to the tree, which often then dies. Fortunately this practice has stopped.

Perhaps the biggest threat to redwoods is from logging, but many areas are now protected, especially within the National Parks. The biggest trees are so tall that if they are felled, the force of them landing on the ground smashes the timber to the extent that it can only be used for less-valuable fencing or matches.

Mulberry

Morus

The mulberry has a stunning form. There was a beautiful one that draped itself over the stone wall in the Gravetye Manor vegetable garden where I used to work. The fruits are an ephemeral delight, almost impossible to market fresh due to their extreme fragility, but worth making a special journey to a known tree at harvest time.

Good for: fruit, silk worms, edible leaves, timber, paper

Though there are more than a hundred known species, the three most common species of mulberry are the white, red and black (*Morus alba*, *M. rubra* and *M. nigra*). The white form is the one used for producing silk, which comes from the cocoon of the silkworm. The larvae are fed mulberry leaves for about six weeks until they start spinning their cocoon.

The white mulberry leaf is also a valuable feed source for livestock and humans. It is very high in protein which makes it useful when integrated into agroforestry systems (see pages 41–2), where trees are included for their browse. In your garden you can harvest a plentiful source of salad leaves by annually pollarding a mulberry and picking the resulting new growth when the leaves are small.

Mulberry trees are dioecious, which means there are separate male and female trees. The pollen from the males is so allergenic that planting them has been banned in some American cities, though of course without them the females will bear no fruit.

A thousand years ago, Buddhist monks of the Khmer Empire of South East Asia used the bark of mulberry trees to make paper. In Japan, a technique using the stems is still employed, turning them into *tengujo*, which is the thinnest paper in the world, so transparent it is often used as a material in lampshades.

Many of the larger plantings of mulberry around the world were undertaken to encourage local production of silk. King James I decided in the 1600s that England needed to develop its own silk industry and ordered thousands of mulberry trees, at the same time putting pressure on other landowners to do the same. Sadly he ordered the wrong species, choosing black instead of white. Not only was this less suitable for the silkworm it was also not well adapted for the English climate at the time, so all in all not a great success.

Persian ironwood

Parrotia persica

Of the many many trees given the name ironwood,
I have highlighted *Parrotia persica*, partly in memory
of a beautiful specimen at a garden I worked at, but also
for its winter flowering and glorious autumn display of
leaves. Add a striking bark texture and you have
a superb ornamental tree.

Good for: timber, ornament

In its native area by the Caspian sea, the hard wood is used for tool handles and building bridges. There are many other quicker-growing trees, however, which means that despite its tough timber it is not grown commercially for its wood. What has made it popular beyond its original habitat is its good looks.

Persian ironwood takes a while to grow to full size, and so is often a great choice for a garden. In autumn the leaves are spectacular, with a range of colours from deep golden yellow to rich dark purplish red. It is related to the witch hazel and has similar flowers in late winter and early spring, providing a splash of red in the bare branches. The bark is lovely too; the technical term for it is 'exfoliating', which means that it naturally sheds thin layers that peel off. This often leads to variations in colour between the older bark and the young fresh layer underneath.

The tree gets its name from Friedrich Parrot (1791–1841), an explorer, physician, botanist and inventor. In the early nineteenth century, when the region was under Russian rule, he led an expedition up Mount Ararat (the first recorded such trip). Though there doesn't seem to be much evidence that he 'discovered' the tree, it seems to have been named to honour him and his work in the geographical area where it originated.

I've done quite a bit of chainsaw work in my years in horticulture, and you get used to the differences between tree species. Cutting soft or slightly rotten woods is so easy it sometimes takes you by surprise and you rarely need to sharpen your chain. At the other end of the spectrum is the Persian ironwood. We had to remove a few low branches on a tree to allow access – just a five minute job, I thought! The wood is so tough it not only blunted the chain but damaged it so badly I had to replace it. How woodworkers managed to craft it before machine tools I have no idea.

Pine

Pinus

Pine is a slightly confusing name, since it is sometimes used as a name for all conifer trees. Here I shall use it to refer to members of the genus *Pinus*, of which there are more than 120. Though typical of colder climates, they are widespread, with one species even surviving on the equator.

Good for: timber, wildlife, ornament, food

Pines have four stages of leaf growth, of which the needle is the one we would usually associate with the tree. Pine trees are members of the class of plants called 'gymnosperms', meaning naked seed. As such, they do not produce flowers or fruits but instead produce seeds in their distinctive female cone. The male cone, which disperses the pollen, is much smaller and only on the tree for a relatively short time, disappearing once it has done its work.

Pine trees are evergreen, meaning they stay green all year round. They do drop their needles but gradually over the whole year as they grow and replace them, rather than all in one go in autumn like deciduous trees. Different species have evolved to survive in a surprisingly wide range of habitats, from the equator to 5,000 m (16,400 ft) up a freezing mountain. This, and the variety of size and forms, have led them to become a popular ornamental species around the world. Some pine trees are grown for cutting, such as Christmas trees, though spruce is also a popular alternative.

The seeds are an important food source for animals and humans, not least in one of my favourite sauces, pesto.

Pines played a part in Darwin's observations of earthworms, still a seminal study relevant to our understanding of soil today. As he sat for days watching earthworms he noticed that they always grabbed the pairs of pine needles by the joined end so they could pull them into their burrows. This led him to hypothesise that they had evolved to behave in this way.

Pines can live a long time, and it is not unusual for them to reach a thousand years old. Of all the species, the bristlecone pine (*Pinus longaeva*) can reach astonishing ages. The Great Basin specimen is nearly 5,000 years old, making it the oldest individual tree in the world. There are other trees that propagate clonally (for instance by sending out suckers that then become new plants) that are older.

Plane

Platanus

Platanus is a small genus of large trees, many of which are sycamores, though confusingly what we in the UK call sycamore, the sycamore maple, belongs to a different family. The London plane is the most common species in cities; coping well with polluted air, it is a key tool in urban planting for health and wellbeing.

Good for: timber, urban planting

Planes have big, maple-like leaves and large, brown fruit-heads that stay on the tree over the winter, making it quite easy to identify. The flaky, grey, camouflage-like bark is also quite distinctive.

Sycamore's main use is for timber. It grows quickly, producing a pale timber with a coarse grain. Oriental plane (also known as Old World sycamore or *Platanus orientalis*) is one of the timbers known as lacewood, since the grain when polished has the appearance of lace. It is used extensively for ornamental woodworking and instrument making.

Because sycamores grow so quickly and are easy to establish, some (especially the occidental or American plane) are being researched for producing biomass for energy and heating.

As we have seen on pages 41–2, trees can filter out pollutants from the air as well as reducing noise pollution and modifying extremes of temperature. Few tree species are better than the London plane at surviving in the clogged atmosphere of our cities, so it is no surprise that it is a popular tree with town planners, despite its relatively poor abilities to support wildlife.

The Buttonwood Agreement was drawn up and signed by the founders of the New York Stock Exchange in 1792, drawing its name from the tree under which it was signed. While the original American sycamore tree (buttonwood is another name for *Platanus occidentalis*) has long since gone, there is a young tree planted on Wall Street to commemorate the historic occasion.

The London plane (*Platanus x hispanica*) is a hybrid between american sycamore and oriental plane. Despite not occurring naturally together, fate brought them together in the mid-seventeenth century in the garden of the botanist and plant hunter John Tradescant the Younger. Once planted near each other, and being closely enough related, they hybridized to form the London plane. It didn't take long to realize that it was a tree well suited to its surroundings, and it has been a mainstay of London streets ever since.

Poplar
Populus

Fast-growing yet relatively durable, poplar has good reason to be popular. The tall, columnar species, useful as a windbreak, are a landscape feature in many European countries. Poplar has also typically been the wood of choice for making matches, and more recently a key species for biomass for energy.

Good for: timber, biomass, windbreaks, livestock feed, wildlife

The most recognizable species are the tall spire-shaped types such as black poplar (*Populus nigra*). These are often planted as windbreaks in sentinel-like lines along field boundaries.

The catkins, or male flowers, which produce clouds of pollen for the wind to waft onto the females, are also a striking feature, with some species producing red or pink catkins up to 10 cm (4 in) long. Also known as cottonwood, it gets its name from the mass of cotton-like white fluff that forms on the female flowers in the early summer.

In ancient Greece, poplar was the wood of choice for shields, and it was preferred to heavier oak even as late as the Middle Ages. Though there is less call now for shield manufacturing, its relative strength and close, straight grain means it is used for many single- or short-use products, such as matches, paper, pallets and even cheese cartons.

Historically, forests of aspen (a subset of the poplar) are

among the most biodiverse habitats, and in particular have a special relationship with beavers. Beavers love aspen and have been recorded travelling further to harvest aspen than other trees. They use the bigger trunks for dams but also adore eating the leaves. In damaged ecosystems with limited food choices and riparian habitats, beavers have been known to harm aspen plantations. However, if they are allowed the space and time they can also be pivotal in restoring those degraded landscapes, slowing river flow, creating bends and providing perfect conditions for aspens to grow: a perfect example of a natural synergistic relationship.

I'm always fascinated by these very specific partnerships that evolution creates. Another one connected with poplar is the aspen hoverfly, native to Scotland and thought to exist only in twelve sites. The larvae of this rare insect rely on dead aspen wood for food. Fewer aspens are being planted and there is a culture of tidiness in woodlands, with some landowners clearing fallen trees rather than leaving them to rot in situ. This destruction of habitat means this tiny symbol of biodiversity is at real risk of extinction.

Cherry

Prunus

No tree list would be complete without the cherry. It is famous around the world, revered in Japan for its magnificent blossom, and the provider of delicious fruit and prized timber. Its place in our culture is reflected in how many traditional and modern songs feature this remarkable tree.

Good for: fruit, timber, wildlife

The most distinctive feature of cherry trees is their ephemeral pink or white blossoms. These are stunning in most species, and a range of ornamental varieties has been bred for even more spectacular displays. Many cherry species have horizontal rings or markings on their bark. The wild cherry (*Prunus avium*) has a smooth, almost shiny, bark between those rings.

There is a large number of cherry species, many of them edible, the two main ones we grow being the sweet cherry (*P. avium* varieties) and the sour cherry (*P. cerasus*). Birds absolutely love cherries, and keeping them from stripping your prized fruit is one of the main challenges in trying to get a crop.

The timber has a fine and even grain, often with a tint of pink or orange to it. It is well behaved when worked. Cherry is a relatively short-lived tree, harvested at between fifty and seventy years old. The trees are not huge and so the timber tends to be used for smaller furniture or flooring.

In parts of Germany and the Czech Republic, the cherry forms a part of the celebrations of St Barbara. Her feast day is on 4 December, and on that day a branch from a cherry tree is cut and put in a vase of water in the house. The branch should come into flower around Christmas. If it blossoms exactly on Christmas Day it is a good omen for the coming year.

Cherries have been a part of our diet for millennia. They are mentioned in the Bible, as well as by ancient Greek and Roman writers. It is thought that Roman soldiers spread the cherry around the Empire as they conquered new lands. The fruit, presumably in dried form, was part of their military rations and they spat the stones out as they marched. There is an old saying that to find the old Roman roads you just need to look for lines of cherry trees that sprouted from those seeds.

Plum

Prunus

I feel the plum is rather underappreciated – neither ubiquitous like apples and oranges nor celebrated like cherries. To see a tree laden to breaking point with fat fruit is one of my summer delights; popping one of the warm ripe fruits straight from the tree into your mouth is pure heaven.

Good for: fruit, woodturning, carving

Mainly cultivated for its fruit, plum also provides valuable timber, which is often beautifully coloured. I turned some bowls from a specimen I saved from a fire, which had fantastic swirls of purple

and yellow. However, since the trunks don't usually grow very long or straight, the timber is not widely used.

Fresh plums, though delicious, are a fleeting seasonal treat. They don't keep long. Indeed, if you don't get them off the tree quickly the wasps and birds will beat you to it. There is a long history of preserving them for year-round eating. Plum jam is delicious, though I find the sweeter dessert plums make a rather bland conserve compared to damsons, which have more flavour and a tartness that I love. Dried plums are called prunes, and can be eaten dried, or rehydrated and stewed. I love dried prunes, but a childhood of school puddings have rather put me off the stewed version.

Though the plum is less acclaimed these days, this was not always the case. In the days before year-round global supplies we were more appreciative of our local fruits. In the UK, 'plum' even became a byword for quality or something really desirable. The people of Pershore in Worcestershire still celebrate the fruit. In August, the whole town is taken over by a month of events, which, in their own words, 'turn the town purple'.

The plum is important in Chinese and Japanese culture. As an early-flowering tree, it has been a symbol of the end of winter and the birth of a new year. In Japan, plums would be planted in the north-eastern part of the garden to provide protection against those evil spirits that come in on the cold winds.

Plums have a powerful laxative effect, celebrated in the naming of one particularly potent variety called 'Shit Smock', which comes from the Forest of Dean, an area of the UK famous for (among other things) its dark sense of humour.

Almond

Prunus amygdalus

Almonds have gained a dubious reputation due
to the way they are grown in drought-prone
California. But if cultivated sustainably, there is
no reason these amazing trees cannot provide a
valuable protein source. And without them, how
will I meet my son's addiction to marzipan?

Good for: nuts, timber

Like many of our fruit and nut trees, the almond is part of the
genus *Prunus*. The bit we eat, though called a nut, is actually the
seed from the fruit. The shell is the outer part of the stone that
protects the seed. This is why an almond in its shell looks like
a peach stone. The tough, fleshy fruits are also edible, though
they need to be picked when young. Called green almonds,
they are a bit sour and often eaten dipped in salt as a snack.

Almond is one of the very first trees to flower in spring, giving
it the nickname of 'tree of life'. This does make it vulnerable to
frosts in cooler climates. Though mostly grown for its edible
part, almond wood has its uses too. It very strong and beautifully
coloured, and used for items such as picture frames and tuning
pegs for musical instruments.

The story of the California almond groves is a typical tale
of human greed and our inability to live within the limits of

our natural resources. The climate in California is well suited to growing almonds, with a relatively hot and dry climate. The state's long agricultural heritage meant it had a good irrigation system to ensure high yields. There are estimated to be more than 7,000 growers of the tree in California, producing around 80 per cent of the world's supply. However, they are grown in intensive monocultures. This not only means that growers have had to import billions of honeybees to ensure pollination, but they also put such a strain on the water supplies that they are contributing to the region's increasing drought problems. Water has become such a challenge that growers are now removing trees and looking for alternative crops with lower irrigation needs. Bad news for American growers, and the climate, but perhaps I will have a market for the crop from the trees we have planted at Eastbrook Farm in south-west England. Though with only six nuts from sixty trees last year, I am not holding my breath.

Pear

Pyrus

Though not quite as easy to cultivate as apples, pears are a fantastic winter fruit. There are many varieties you can pick hard and store cold, bringing them out to ripen and eat as you need them. Perry (pear cider) is an environmentally friendly tipple, with a more refined taste than most ciders.

Good for: fruit, timber, wildlife

Most commonly grown for its edible fruit, the pear is closely related to the apple and grows in a similar way. In commercial orchards it is most often grafted onto a quince root. Using these compatible but less vigorous rootstocks results in a smaller tree that fruits more quickly, handy for quicker return on investment and easier picking.

Perry pears are a small, hard type of pear used for making perry (sometimes also called pear cider). Sparkling perry has often been used as an alternative to Champagne and has a relatively low carbon footprint. Since the trees can be shaken and the fallen fruit harvested from the ground, perry pears are usually grown on a more vigorous root and can become very big – up to 20 m (65 ft) – and can live and produce heavy crops for up to 300 years. Having fallen out of fashion, there is currently a small revival in the popularity of perry, and I am a big fan, having planted a few hundred trees five years ago and hoping to grow more.

Though native to China and Asia, the pear had reached Greece by the time of Homer and in the first century AD Pliny the Elder listed forty-one varieties that the Romans were cultivating. The empire enabled the northward spread of fruit growing and propagation, and pears became popular particularly in France and England, since they could thrive here where many other more tender fruits could not. However, it was from the seventeenth century that the breeding was done that laid the foundation for our modern softer and sweeter varieties.

There are so many stories and myths involving pears that it is obvious it has held a vital place in many cultures, particularly in cooler climates with fewer native fruits and cold winters. It seems that in modern times we have become so used to importing fruit from around the globe all year round that a tree that was once so crucial for our sustenance has been overshadowed by more glamorous newcomers.

Oak

Quercus

Oak is a favourite around the world, shaped like a child's drawing of a tree. We have used its hard and durable wood for thousands of years to make all sorts of things from ships to houses to furniture. It supports an astonishing range of organisms and can even provide protein for human consumption from the acorns.

Good for: food, timber, wildlife

Oak is probably most well known as a building material, we use it for the structural parts of houses and boats. It is not only strong but, due to tyloses in its cells, it takes a long time to rot even when untreated. This makes it particularly useful for boats and when making barrels to store liquids in. Oak timber is also workable and versatile with a lovely grain and colour when polished, and so is also popular as a wood for furniture makers

The acorn, the nut of the oak, holds a special place in our hearts, a potent symbol that something tiny can grow into a mighty thing of beauty. Acorns are also high in protein (typically 6 per cent). Pannage is an ancient practice where farmers take their pigs through oak forests to glean the fallen acorns. Humans can also eat acorns, though we usually grind them up first to make flour. Acorn flour is becoming more available and can be added at 50 per cent to a bread mix for a super earthy flavour. If you are making your own acorn flour,

be sure to wash out some of the tannins from the acorns before grinding to avoid an upset stomach.

Well over 2,000 species of organisms are linked to oak trees, including insects, birds and fungi. They are a cornerstone of biodiversity, just one more reason they are so revered and loved. They have evolved to survive and often will lose quite large branches (for instance, when struck by lightning) but regrow from the trunk. This gives them a thick solid base that won't fall down even in the strongest gales. The Penchanga Great Oak in Temecula, California, is reputed to be the oldest oak alive, at an estimated age of 2,000 years, though there are many others around the world that are many hundreds of years old, including the Major Oak in Sherwood Forest, which, according to legend, provided a hiding spot for Robin Hood.

Mangrove
Rhizophora

Mangroves are a truly remarkable group of trees able to
thrive in the brackish salty water where the sea meets the
land. They form a tangled mass of roots and trees, also called
mangroves, or sometimes mangrove swamps or forests.
By growing together in this way they are able to withstand
the ebb and flow of the tide and coastal storms.

Good for: timber, dyeing and tanning, livestock feed,
wildlife, climate mitigation

Technically, only about half of the species known as mangroves
belong to the 'true' mangrove genus of *Rhizophora*. Though
many species are more like shrubs growing to about 20 m
(65 ft), some will grow to considerable size. For instance, in
West Africa they can reach 60 m (200 ft). Not surprisingly for
a tree adapted to wet conditions, their bark and leaves are shiny
and smooth to repel as much water as possible.

The timber of the mangrove is perfectly adapted for boat
building, and of course it is in plentiful supply exactly where it is
needed. However, the wood is also used for making houses, as
well as for fuel.

Most mangroves only grow in tropical and subtropical
climates, since they cannot cope with freezing temperatures,
but despite being a very small proportion of the world's trees
(only 1 per cent of tropical forests), they play a crucial role in

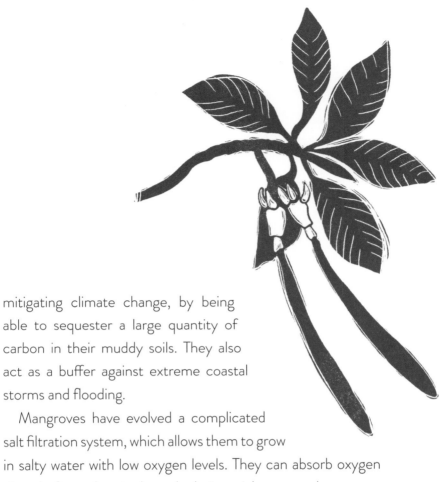

mitigating climate change, by being able to sequester a large quantity of carbon in their muddy soils. They also act as a buffer against extreme coastal storms and flooding.

Mangroves have evolved a complicated salt filtration system, which allows them to grow in salty water with low oxygen levels. They can absorb oxygen directly from the air through their aerial roots and can even store these gases within their roots to use when the water levels rise and cut off the air supply.

Mangroves have an ingenious way of ensuring their seed survives and grows. Unlike normal trees, which drop a dormant seed that can survive until the conditions are right for germination, the mangrove seed germinates while still attached to its mother. It then grows either in the fruit, or pops out through it. This fruit is buoyant and able to float off with the growing seedling until it can root into some suitable seaside mud. Amazingly, it can survive in this state for more than a year.

Black Locust

Robinia pseudoacacia

Super vigorous, hardy and thorny, the black locust is considered an invasive species in many places, even in some areas of the United States where it is native. However, its ability to fix nitrogen and the durability of its timber could make it a star performer in our fight against climate change.

Good for: timber, livestock feed, wood fuel, wildlife, bee food in honey production

Black locust is easy to identify when in flower, with its highly scented racemes of (usually) white blossoms. It also has very long, vicious spines on its younger growth, a useful armour against browsing animals as it establishes. *Robinia* is able to send suckers up from the roots to form new trees, so in areas where the understory is not managed you may see new shoots coming up around the trunk. This ability to spread is what makes it invasive, but it can be helpful in establishing new plantations, especially in areas with poor soil, where other trees are slower to get going.

There are mixed reports about its use as animal fodder. The American silvopastoralist Steve Gabriel cites it as one of his top four trees for supporting livestock, though he does recognize that animals need to become accustomed to eating it. It also seems that while young leaves can be eaten with no problems, old dry leaves with higher tannin levels can be toxic.

Robinia wood is extremely hard. Check out hardness ratings for woods on the Janka Hardness Test, which measures how much force you need to exert to force a steel ball into the timber. Black locust scores about 1,700 lbf (7,560 Newtons). This is significantly harder than many oaks and mahoganies. There is a joke among American farmers that goes 'How do you know when it's time to replace your black locust fence posts? Pop a stone on top of the post and when the stone rots it time to put some new posts in.'

Robinia is an opinion divider, to the extent that a 2017 study recounting how it has spread in Central Europe has the title 'Black Locust – beloved and despised', highlighting both its commercial benefits alongside its power in remediation and erosion control, but also the role it may be playing in outcompeting less vigorous native species with potential knock-on impacts on wildlife.

Willow

Salix

Willow is one of the most remarkable trees. It is able to grow in the wettest ground and it brings health and vigour to other plants and animals. Salicylic acid (also known as aspirin) in willow tissue can cure headaches, help plants to fight disease and even make your tomatoes sweeter.

Good for: timber, Livestock feed, wildlife, tanning, medicine, weaving material

Willow has so many uses it is impossible to cover them all here. It is a fast-growing and pliable species that responds well to coppicing. Not strong enough for buildings but great for making hurdles and famously cricket bats, willow is also a perfect weaving material, traditionally for baskets, but more recently it has become popular for outdoor sculptures.

Willow is also a crucial species for feeding livestock in agroforestry systems, as the high levels of micronutrients, tannins and salicylic acid in the leaves improve animal health. Indeed, it is common for animals to self-medicate by seeking out willow when they are feeling unwell.

I was involved in a cider orchard trial in which the trees were mulched with willow woodchip. As the salicylic acid leached from the freshly chipped material, it was taken up by the trees and seemed to stimulate an immune response in the plants, which reduced scab levels.

My old horticultural lecturer, the great Oliver Menhinick, used to say about willow that it was so tough it would 'root in your pocket if you leave it there long enough'. While he had probably seen the amount of dirt in my pocket, willow does have an incredible ability to grow. Willow water (obtained by soaking willow wood in water) can be used as a rooting agent to help more relectutact species to succeed.

As a musician I am always excited when that part of my world collides with my day job. Some of the earliest whistles may well have been fashioned from willow, which is soft and pliable and relatively easy to shape and carve holes into.

Willows do like a lot of water, and if you plant them too near your house there is a risk they will grow their roots into your drainage system in search of moisture. As the roots expand this can crack and break the drains. So unless you have enough space to keep the tree at least 100 m (330 ft) away I wouldn't recommend it for your garden.

Elder

Sambucus

With species found almost all over the world, this is one of the most iconic small trees. It thrives in a range of habitats, producing fragrant edible flowers that are often made into cordials. The elder has an almost mythical standing in many cultures, and even made it into Harry Potter, as the wood of the Deathly Hallows wand.

Good for: food, medicine, wildlife, dyes, keeping the devil away

Elders do not grow big, rarely exceeding 20 m (65 ft), and they seed readily. Birds love their berries, and disperse the seed far and wide in their droppings. The flowers are white or cream and often form large, flat clusters. They have a powerful and distinct scent and taste that has long been used to flavour drinks. The alcoholic drink sambuca, which took its name, though mostly aniseed-flavoured, does include elderflower.

Most of the plant is toxic. The exception is the black, or sometimes red, berries which, despite being poisonous to most mammals when raw, are delicious when cooked. The seeds are not safe, however, so should be removed. In the days before industrial dyes, the elder was a useful source for many colours: the bark produces greys and black, the leaves yellow and green, and the deep hues of the berry give blue or purple.

The elder has a long association with the devil, which is perhaps why J.K. Rowling chose it for her Deathly Hallows wand. The

wood is terrible as firewood, making the fire spit, which was thought to be work of the devil. However, if you planted an elder outside your house or stable, or hung branches by the door, this was reputed to keep the devil away.

There are additional stories of witches being able to turn themselves into elder trees, and even in Danish mythology of the trees being able to get up and walk. The cutting of elders was prohibited, and care was taken never to make a baby's cradle from elder wood, in case the witch came back to life and attacked the child.

One special property of the elder is its hollow stem. Both the Latin and the common names refer to this characteristic. The name elder supposedly derived from *aeld*, the Anglo-Saxon word for 'fire'. The stems were used to blow air on the embers as a rudimentary bellows. Meanwhile, *Sambucus* is from the Greek word *sambukē*, which is a musical whistle made from the twigs.

Sorbus

Sorbus

Sorbus is a big genus with more than 100 species of trees and shrubs. The most well known are probably the red or orange berried rowan (*S. aucuparia*), and the whitebeam (*S. aria*), with its pale underleaf. I have a soft spot for the wild service (*S. torminalis*). The fruit of most species is edible, though not necessarily delicious.

Good for: fruit, timber, wildlife

The fruit is small and often brightly coloured, edible to humans and a valuable food source for a range of wildlife, as it lasts well on the tree late into winter. In German it is even called the

Vogelbeerbaum or 'bird berry tree'. The berries from wild service, which are only about 1.5 cm (1/2 in) in diameter used to be given to children as sweets, while those from the rowan make a vivid-coloured jelly. The time it takes to harvest them means they are now mostly neglected as a human delicacy, so finding wild service trees is often the sign of an ancient woodland.

The timber from *Sorbus* is hard and not prone to splitting. In particular, wild service wood was historically prized for tool and weapon handles as well as for a variety of furniture and musical instruments. It was so strong that it was even used as wheel axles and cogs in mill machinery.

Sorbus is particularly prone to apomixis (reproduction in plants without fertilization), which is one reason for its genetic diversity. Delving into this diversity you find some remarkable stories, not least where I live in the South West of England. In Gloucestershire alone there are thought to be at least six species of whitebeam not found anywhere else in the world. One of them, The Ship Rock whitebeam (*S. parviloba*), exists as one lonely specimen clinging to a rock in the Forest of Dean.

In contrast, the rowan or mountain ash (*S. aucuparea*) is widely found and held dear in folklore. In Norse mythology it is the tree used to make the first woman, perhaps due to its relatively small size and slender form, contrasted with the more substantial ash tree that was supposedly the origin of men.

Rowan wood was thought to ward off evil magic. This was adopted by some early Christians who believed that the Cross was made from rowan, and would fashion small crosses from rowan twigs to protect buildings and animals.

Elm

Ulmus

Once a common site in many temperate regions of the world their numbers have sadly been decimated in recent decades by Dutch Elm Disease. Resistant breeding programmes give some optimism that we may once again see these giants of the landscape in greater numbers.

Good for: timber, wildlife livestock fodder

Timber from elm doesn't split easily when nailed or screwed, so it was popular for making timber-framed buildings. Many of the barns in the UK are made of elm, as documented so brilliantly in Robert J. Somerville's book *Barn Club*. It is also relatively easy to shape (when steamed) and so has traditionally been used to make wheels, chairs and baskets.

The leaves, especially that of the wych elm, are easily confused with hazel. They provide food not only for domesticated animals but also for a range of wild creatures, including the white letter hairstreak butterfly, which breeds exclusively on elm. Birds also eat elm seeds.

Elm flowers are one of the earliest of the tree blossoms and appear before the leaves, giving the trees a pink haze at the crown. The fruits are small 'samaras', the name given to fruits or nuts that have wings, for example on ash and maple trees.

Most elm is classified as a soft hardwood, and will rot quickly if left outside. It even has a reputation for dropping whole branches from the tree without warning which, as well as being a popular wood for coffins, has led to elm being associated with death. However, when permanently wet, elm wood is very resistant to rotting. Until the seventeenth century, in the days before metal and plastic piping, hollowed elm trunks were used in Europe as water pipes. Examples of these can still be found in the Science Museum in London.

Brighton & Hove in the South East of England has the national elm collection, with more than 17,000 specimens. This incredible biological assortment includes what are thought to be the largest and oldest English elms (*Ulmus procera*) in the whole of Europe. The pair, nicknamed the Preston Twins, are growing in Preston Park and measure nearly 7 m (23 ft) in circumference. They have been pollarded in the past so are not so tall as they would have been if grown as a single stem, but are believed to be at least 400 years old.

TREE IDENTIFICATION

Being able to spot a *Betula pendula* at a hundred yards may not be an essential life skill for most of us. Nonetheless, I love being able to identify trees when out walking in the woods, or strolling round a garden. There are some obvious things to look out for, such as leaves and flowers, but being able to distinguish subtler signs, such as bud colour and arrangement, will really help narrow down species, particularly during winter, when many trees have no leaves, flowers or fruit. Like any skill in life, the more you practice the better you will get.

Looking from a distance

The overall size and shape of a tree can be a big clue. It might even be the easiest way to recognize some species. A particular feature may appear only at certain times of year. For instance, elm flowers come out in very early spring before their own leaves or those of other deciduous trees have emerged. This gives the elm trees a pinkish hue that can be tricky to distinguish when at ground level looking up but, once you get your eye in, is unmistakable from a distance.

Looking at where the trees are growing can also narrow down your options. If it is next to a river, or in heavy wet soil, species like alder, willow, dogwoods and birches are more likely.

Looking up close

Once you are next to the tree you can start a more detailed examination. Leaf size and shape, flowers, bark and buds are all really good pointers.

Let's take a look at leaves. Are they needles (like a Christmas tree), scaly (such as cedars) or flat (most deciduous trees)? If they are flat does the tree have single leaves, like for instance sycamore, or are there lots on each stalk such as ash? You can look at how the leaves are arranged on the branch. Do the leaves sprout from opposite buds, or do they alternate along the stem? As an example, many willows and dogwoods look very similar in winter when they are bare, and both come in a range of colours that make it tricky to tell the difference in that way. However, willow has buds alternately along the stem while dogwood's buds sit opposite each other. Even in winter, when trees have shed their summer mantle, there might be remnants of their leaves left on the ground to give you a hint.

The shape of the leaves also marks some species out. Maple leaves have a classic shape with their three lobes, as depicted on the Canadian flag. Similarly oak is distinctive, with multiple lobes, though the shape of these lobes varies between the different oak species. Many willows have long thin leaves, but not all of them; goat willow (*Salix caprea*) has a much rounder leaf.

Many trees have similar-shaped leaves, however, so sometimes you have to delve a bit deeper. Check out the edge (also called the margin) of the leaf. Is it smooth or serrated? From a distance ash and rowan leaves look similar, but up close the smooth edges of the ash are easily differentiated from the toothed rowan.

Flowers and berries are another great way to identify a tree, if you happen to be there at the right time of year. One of my favourites is the spindle tree, with its spectacular pink fruits and vivid orange seeds inside. In spring, keep your eyes out for the catkins and tiny red flowers of the hazel, or the marvellous, fluffy, juvenile male flowers of the pussy willow. Alder has fruits that look like tiny little cones from which the miniscule seeds are blown out by wind or washed away by the rain.

The bark might also provide some pointers, though you will likely need more time to get your eye in. There are some real giveaways, like silver birch, with its almost white trunks, which peel off in transparent paper-thin layers. As well as colour, bark texture can be a clue. Cherries, for instance, have horizontal rings or marking around the bark, forming ridges. Make sure you look all the way up the trunk; juvenile and mature bark can be very different.

I'm sure that many purists will eschew using smartphone apps for identification. However, I find they are a great tool for building knowledge and confidence, as well as for engaging kids in looking at trees. Just make sure you are not relying on the app to do all the work for you. I try to do the identification first and then turn to the phone for confirmation.

TREES AND THE ECONOMY

BUY WOOD TO SAVE THE WORLD

How do we make diverse, wildlife-rich woodlands and treescapes profitable? Farmers are beginning to see the benefits of more trees, but product development and public demand for wood products need to catch up. Let's revitalize traditional woodworking crafts and use the latest technology to produce things made from wood. If you want to work with trees, there are so many opportunities at the moment from forestry, agroforestry and carpentry right through to cutting edge polymer development. Wherever you live, you can work with trees or timber and help to retree the world.

It seems counterintuitive to advocate chopping down trees in order to solve climate change. We should, of course, still be reducing our overall consumption, but there are strong reasons to be looking at replacing many materials with wood. The potential benefits are overwhelming. Provided we are not felling ancient trees and forests, but sourcing from an ethical and sustainable system, using wood is a great long-term solution for the planet.

Plastics

Plastic has become the go-to material for most items over the last few decades, and it's easy to see why. It's cheap, lightweight and can be moulded into any shape. However, we are now fully aware of the damage that plastic pollution is causing and of the fact that we should be leaving oil in the ground. Plant-based plastics (including from trees themselves) solve the latter problem, but we also need to perfect truly biodegradable plastics. Until we do that, wood can offer a properly eco alternative. To transform a tree to a wooden product usually just requires some cutting and sanding, while turning plants into plastics takes more energy and usually some chemical treatment. There are already packaging and fabric products on the market that use wood fibre instead of plastic. Give feedback to suppliers that sell to you in plastic or excessive packaging, and when looking for your next chair or shelf, think wood!

The simple chopping board

Here is an example of how a rush to embrace a new technology or material can have unintended consequences. For centuries wood was the only material to make a chopping board from.

It is tough, durable and doesn't blunt your knife. Plastic comes along: it's lighter and seems cleaner. In many countries professional food preparers are obliged to use plastic, often colour-coded for different food types. However, researchers tested the numbers of bacteria on cleaned wooden and plastic boards and found that the wooden boards always had fewer, whether they were used or not. Wood contains antimicrobial chemicals that help to kill bacteria.

Building houses

Wooden houses are nothing new, but in some countries (and, yes, the UK is one of those) we seem very reluctant to embrace wood-framed building, despite the fact that it is often cheaper and easier to construct, as well as sequestering such large amounts of carbon. In many parts of the country we also have strict planning regulations that require new houses to look like old ones. One solution is to replace brick components with wood fibre-based materials. Mixing in woodchips as a part of the aggregate creates a product often known as woodcrete. This material is lighter than traditional building blocks, so it not only helps the climate by reducing the mining for mineral components, but it also takes less fuel to cart the blocks around.

Sourcing wood

How can you be sure that you are buying wood or wooden products from genuinely sustainable sources? It's no good sequestering a bit of carbon if you have contributed to the extinction of rare tree species, or the destruction of a vital ecosystem. The first thing to look at is the FSC (Forestry Stewardship Council) logo. This is a globally recognized standard showing that the product meets a range of environmental and social criteria. Avoid teak, mahogany and ebony, as well as wood from a long list of less famous but equally important and endangered trees. Check out the Wood Database created by Eric Meier for more information (www.wood-database.com).

Wood with a story

It is even more satisfying to find local woodworkers and timber merchants from which to source your wood and wooden products. Though currently likely to be more expensive, this may change as global demand for wood increases, resulting in an increase in the cost of imported wood. Check out social media for people doing really interesting stuff. I love what Patrick Turk is doing with his company Forest2Furniture. Working mostly in and around Sherwood Forest (yes, where Robin Hood lived), he selects amazing old trees that have already fallen or been damaged by storms. He then mills them to sell on to specialist markets.

WORKING WITH TREES

If, like me, you feel deeply connected to trees, what could be better than being paid to work with them? The good news is that there are plenty of opportunities to do just that. Whatever your background or academic qualifications, there are ways of getting into arboricultural work. Here are just a few of the types of jobs out there for tree lovers.

Tree surgeon

This mostly involves pruning or removing trees. Though this might be seen as a destructive profession, a skilled and knowledgeable tree surgeon can make the difference between an ugly butchered tree and a balanced natural looking specimen. This is a physically demanding career, particularly when it involves climbing.

Tree nursery

Most governments around the world are now trying to hit ambitious tree-planting targets. There are big openings for tree nurseries to produce the necessary planting stock. Native trees from locally collected seeds, and specialist grafted stock for productive tree farming systems, are just a couple of the areas to look at.

Orchard growing

If you love trees and food, then maybe consider going into fruit growing. Modern orchard growing combines science and sophisticated machinery with more traditional pruning and observational skills. There are always opportunities for picking fruit during the harvest season to see whether you like it. I first got bitten by the horticulture bug picking grapes in northern Italy.

Woodworking

Making things out of wood is highly satisfying and encompasses a whole range of enterprises, such as woodturning, carpentry, hurdle making, basket weaving and even barn building. The climate benefits of replacing carbon-intensive materials with wood are now recognized, and we are likely to need many more people who understand how to produce useful items from trees.

Forestry and woodland management

Managing forests to get optimum timber yield while maintaining good biodiversity is the challenge facing the twenty-first century, and one that will need a range of bright people with varied skills. A quick look at the UK Forestry Commision jobs page at the time of writing showed the following opportunities: ranger, incentives development officer and a wellbeing advisor.

Agroforestry

Coming back to my own area of work, increasingly farmers are wanting to plant more trees on their land, but they don't necessarily want to plant or manage those trees themselves. I believe there will be huge potential for part- and full-time careers looking after productive trees on other people's farms.

ACKNOWLEDGMENTS

My professional love of trees started with growing apples and pears in various jobs. This flame of passion was nurtured and sustained by some key tree mentors: Katie Butler taught me how to prune; Hugh Ermen showed me the wonders of own-root fruit trees; Matthew Wilson demonstrated how to make it all work in the commercial world.

As I have immersed myself into the world of agroforestry I have been inspired and supported by fellow pioneers. They are too many to mention but their expertise and enthusiasm have been invaluable. On the shoulders of giants!

I am particularly grateful to Helen Browning and Paul Clark, to whom this book is dedicated. Together we strive at Eastbrook Farm on our ambitious and experimental agroforestry project. Thank you Helen for your vision and commitment, and Paul for your indomitable spirit and humour, and both for your unending personal support.

Thank you as always to Monica for making this book happen.

And of course, I am so lucky to have a wonderful family; Ruth, Ivan, and Jonah, who let me slope off to my shed to scribble.

INDEX

Further Reading

Roger Deakin *Wildwood: A Journey Through Trees* (Penguin, 2008)

Giono, Jean *The Man Who Planted Trees* (Peter Owen, 2008)

Li, Qing *Forest Bathing: How Trees Can Help You Find Health and Happiness* (Penguin, 2018).

Raskin, Ben *The Woodchip Handbook* (Chelsea Green Publishing, 2021).

Raskin, Ben & Osborne, Simone (eds) *The Agroforestry Handbook* (The Soil Association, 2019).

Silver, Akiva *Trees of Power: Ten Essential Arboreal Allies* (Chelsea Green Publishing, 2019).

Simard, Suzanne *Finding the Mother Tree: Discovering the Wisdom of the Forest* (Random House, 2021).

Somerville, Robert J. *Barn Club: A Tale of Forgotten Elm Trees, Traditional Craft and Community Spirit* (Chelsea Green Publishing, 2021)

Walter, Robin *Regenerative Forestry: Forestry and Forests for the Future* (The Soil Association, 2022).

Cool Temperate – **cooltemperate.co.uk**
Trees and information inspired by Hugh Ermen, especially on own-root fruit trees.

Orange Pippin Trees – **orangepippintrees.co.uk**
For lots more information on fruit trees, including growing own-root fruit trees.

Wood Database – **wood-database.com**
A comprehensive guide to different kinds of wood, their properties and how sustainable they are.

Ben Raskin is the Head of Horticulture and Agroforestry at the Soil Association in the UK, and author of *Zero Waste Gardening* (2021). He also manages a pioneering agroforestry planting on a 600-hectare (1,480-acre) farm in the South West of England. Ben got the gardening bug while working on an organic vineyard in northern Italy, and has worked in horticulture for thirty years, including a stint as Assistant Head Gardener at the UK charity Garden Organic. He has also written *The Community Gardening Handbook*, *Compost*, *Grow* and *Bees, Bugs & Butterflies* for Leaping Hare Press.

Rosanna Morris has worked in the realm of print for well over ten years. She first got excited about relief print at eighteen during her foundation diploma at the Bristol School of Art. During the course she took a trip to Paris where she encountered huge relief wheat pastes around the city. Once home she wanted to make her drawings big and began carving huge life size woodcuts of British farming and pasted them on abandoned walls around the city. She went on to study Illustration at Camberwell School of Art, where she developed her own unique style, evoking the traditional feel of British Wood Engravings within the aesthetic of contemporary illustration.

The Soil Association is the charity that joins forces with nature for a better future, a world with good health, in balance with nature and a safe climate. Working with everyone to transform the way we eat, farm and care for our natural world, we build real solutions from the ground up. Join us. Together, we are a force for nature. **soilassociation.org**